OPERATION DISEMBROIL

Operation Disembroil

Deception and Escape, Normandy 1940

by

W. H. Dothie

ROBERT HALE · LONDON

© *W. H. Dothie 1985*
First published in Great Britain 1985

Robert Hale Limited
Clerkenwell House
Clerkenwell Green
London EC1R 0HT

Dothie, W.H.
  Operation disembroil: deception and escape,
  Normandy 1940.
  1. Great Britain. *Army*—History   2. World
  War, 1939-1945—Campaigns—France   3. World
  War, 1939-1945—Personal narratives, British
  I. Title
  940.5454′21′0924   D761

ISBN 0-7090-2200-X

Photoset in Palatino by
Kelly Typesetting Limited
Bradford-on-Avon, Wiltshire
Printed in Great Britain by
St Edmundsbury Press
Bury St Edmunds, Suffolk
Bound by Woolnough Bookbinding Limited

Contents

Maps

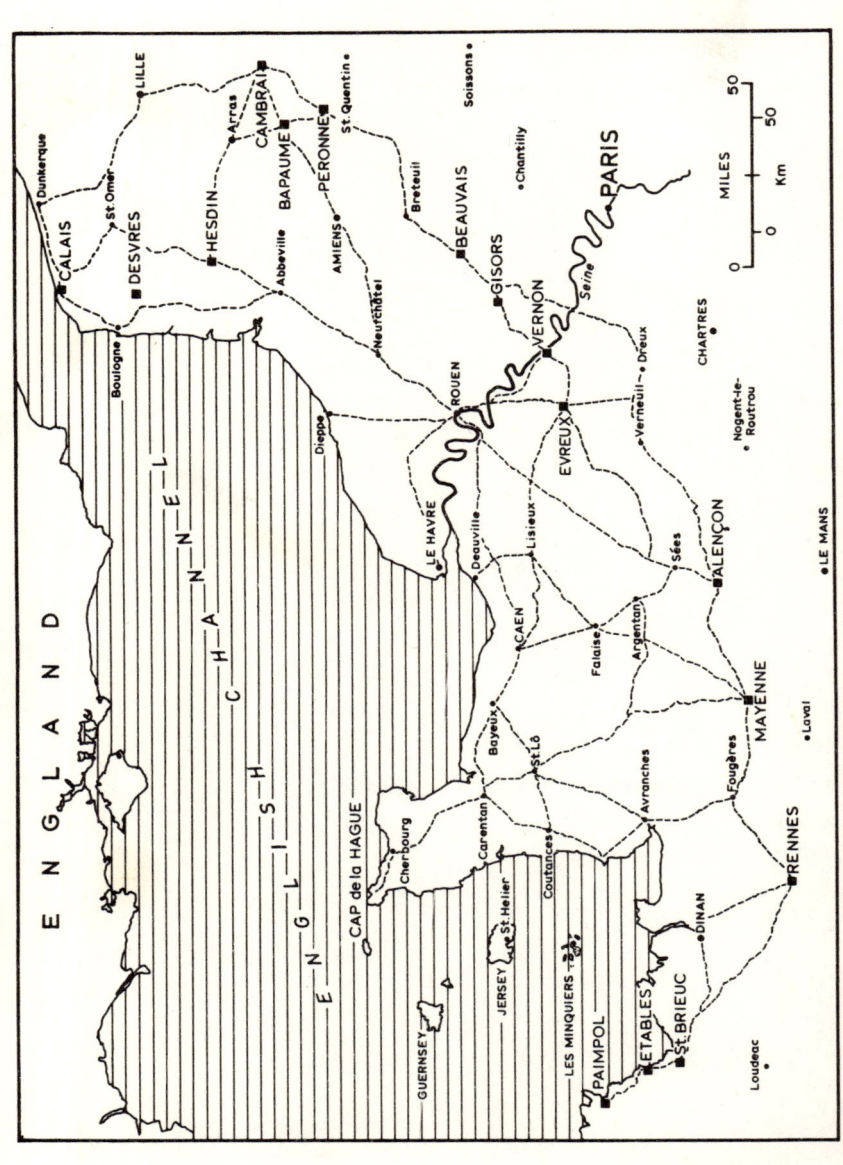

Map showing northern France and the English coastline

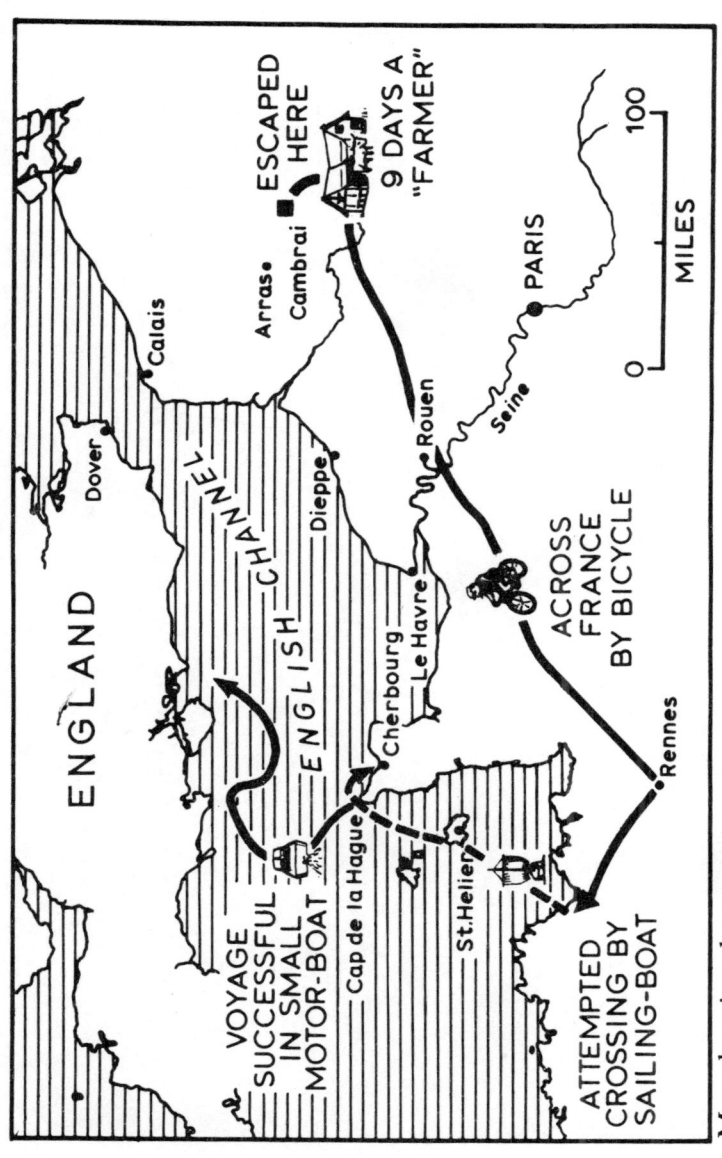

Map showing the escape route

Occupation of the Municipal Farm, Calais

Following the German invasion of Holland and Belgium early in May 1940, units of the British and French Armies advanced across the northern frontier of France into Belgium. At this time I was a Lieutenant in command of an Anti-aircraft Searchlight Troop deployed north of Lille, which consisted of six operational detachments plus a Headquarter detachment. The detachments were stationed at roughly two mile intervals, and their total strength was about 96 men.

Almost immediately, however, came news of the German breakthrough at Sedan, some miles to the south, and the blitzkrieg advance of their armoured spearheads into the French interior. No preparations had been made for defence against attack from this direction and soon

11

emergency orders came to us for a rush move south to defend the Canal du Nord between La Bassee and Bethune. Our instructions were to hold, at all costs, the bridges at La Bassee and Quinchy against attack from the south.

Only one of our number, a Sergeant, had had any previous war experience. The reactions of the rest of us in this period of waiting and wondering were perhaps surprising. Although we knew nothing of the enemy's whereabouts, and had only rumours for news, the general feeling was not of fear, but of intense curiosity. The wildest rumours circulated however, and from the local gendarmes we learnt that a number of suspected fifth columnists had been arrested. Otherwise, apart from aerial activity and the strange atmosphere of deserted villages, there was no evidence of the enemy's existence.

The bridge at Quinchy turned out to be non-existent, having been demolished since our map was issued. That at La Bassee, however, proved to be a fine new single-span concrete structure with a little inn at the side of the southern approach road; the inn-keeper was a cheerful soul who did not reckon much for the possibilities of invasion. As for the Bosche coming from the south—that was 'Rigolo! Ha! Ha!'

The exact means of carrying out our orders to hold the bridge caused considerable concern to Battery HQ, and orders were constantly changed and countermanded, which made for as much debate as activity. Before any real action started, however, we received orders to move again, this time to Calais: we were very disappointed—and little knew what we should run into there. The journey took several days, and soon became a nightmare, traffic on the road forming into a solid mass which moved only in fits and starts. Before long complete chaos seemed to reign everywhere.

Then the second in command of our Battery appeared with yet new instructions. A rough holding scheme had been mapped out allotting areas and sites to the four Troops in the Battery; each Troop was to drive direct to its area, set up a Headquarters, arrange accommodation and set up ground defences. Then the Troop Commander was to report to the Battery OC at a rendezvous in a suburb of Calais for a conference and further orders.

We were given maps, and my Troop found its way to its designated location, a small village called Marcq on the main road between Calais and Dunkirk, just east of Calais, without difficulty. My first concern on arrival was to find a building large enough to hold all our 96 strong unit, together with convenient parking close by for all our transport vehicles. The map showed a farm, the 'Ferme Municipale', in the centre of our area, which looked as if it might be suitable, and halting the convoy on the road nearby, I went ahead to examine it. As I drove through the entrance gates, a civilian appeared and said everything was ready and I could take over at once. Apart from him I never saw anyone connected with the farm and when I later looked for him he had disappeared, possibly in a light aeroplane which took off from a nearby racing track. All very odd!

The place was ideal, as it turned out, for my purpose, with ample barns and numerous outhouses, all in excellent condition. Hardly believing my luck, I soon had everyone installed. In the barns, there were ample supplies of straw for the palliasses. There was firewood for cooking. Water taps were in working order and there was plenty of parking space for the vehicles. No doubt because it was the Calais Municipal Farm, the place was extremely well maintained, and the offices, which faced directly on to the entrance drive, made excellent headquarters. They also provided me with sleeping accommodation, which had every modern convenience, including radio, telephone and electricity, all working. The telephone was very soon bristling with indignant calls from the office of the Mayor demanding an explanation for our unwarranted intrusion: I said I would come in and explain, when I could get to Calais; needless to say, when I did get there I found no-one in the least interested.

It was about the 23rd May, three or four days after our arrival at these comfortable quarters, that German tanks reached Calais, and communications with our Battery HQ ceased completely. It still seemed the sensible thing to comply with the order to install ourselves here, and to hold it in conjunction with the other detachments deployed at sites about two miles apart. Hopefully, someone somewhere knew we were doing so.

Our strength at the farm was soon swelled by large numbers of French and Belgian army stragglers who came in, and also by some twenty or so men from detachments of the Queen Victoria Rifles and the Rifle Brigade who had lost touch with their own units. They had been rushed by ship to Calais as last minute reinforcements only a day or so previously, but had been unable to find their motor cycles and equipment when disembarked. We had no problems with rations for I had sent several parties foraging into Calais, all of which had obtained supplies from various depots there; and we also had a quantity of consumable stores which had been left with us soon after we arrived at the Farm by units passing on their way to the port for embarkation.

I also found I had somehow acquired a new subaltern as second in command of the troop; I suggested to him (mainly to keep him occupied) that he might try to organise the military refugees and stragglers, who by now were streaming along the road in increasing numbers, past the farm and in many cases coming in, into some form of defensive force, for which we had ample accommodation and rations. When next I ran him down I found that he had certainly got cracking. The whole farm was seething with French and Belgian soldiers, all busy cooking over camp fires and generally making themselves at home.

Among these Flemish-speaking Belgians I located a sergeant who spoke a French that I could recognise; and through him I managed to get parties organised to collect arms discarded along the road and distribute them among the men. The haul included light machine guns as well as rifles.

At the time I did not stop to think whether this activity would be of any use: it just seemed the right and natural thing to do, and at the end of the day I felt reasonably pleased at what we had achieved. Later however, when the new subaltern and I were turning in for bed, I was worried by something which I noticed as we were undressing: his back was completely covered with whip scars, neatly and evenly spread, as cat o'ninetails would have been. I began then to ponder on his status rather carefully, realising somewhat belatedly that he had appeared on the scene from nowhere, without any papers or other authorisation from either Battery or Regimental HQ, and I decided to investigate him on the following day.

Evidence of fifth-column activity was certainly not lacking; we saw apparently French priests in their robes chatting to French troops, and on one occasion a theatrical-looking Scottish soldier, complete in piper's regalia with sporran, kilt and pipes, all by himself. At the time I did not react as I might have done normally, because of the tense atmosphere and my necessary preoccupation with more urgent problems. Afterwards it became clear that many of the strange-looking characters we saw were part of the army of fifth-columnists that descended on the locality during the Blitzkrieg.

These odd events and mysterious visitors added to the already growing tension felt by everyone in our little garrison. And disturbing rumours of colossal new German tanks, carrying heavy guns and armour plate that was proof against any anti-tank shell, and of deadly dive-bombers that pin-pointed their target with fiendish noise and accuracy, brought in presently by white-faced stragglers, spread anxiety even deeper through all ranks.

Then we heard the thundering crashes and detonations of an artillery duel between German heavy guns and the British naval force off Calais, and saw huge columns of thick black smoke rising from the direction of the harbour. The noise of the barrage was like giant dustbins being banged around in a sunken courtyard.

After a while, there was another distant sound—that of tank engines revving up; and we saw Very lights rising and falling on the ridge of hills that lies some 4 or 5 miles inland from the coast. It seemed that German tanks were making a somewhat slower and more methodical approach to our location than we had expected. But they were definitely coming.

It was now late morning; I warned all NCO's to be ready to put the emergency plan we had prepared into operation as soon as I gave the signal. The Municipal Farm buildings were hopelessly exposed to attack from all sides as well as from the air. But about a hundred yards away was the entrance to a smaller private farm in the middle of a wood, and I had decided that this should be our reserve HQ. It was approached by a narrow lane with a gated entrance which could easily be blocked up, thus sealing the perimeter against tank attack. Meanwhile, all our heavy equipment and searchlights had been made unservicable. I gave these proceedings a start by recklessly putting a sledge-hammer through the 4 foot diameter concave mirror of a searchlight.

As soon as shells started falling on the farm buildings, I gave the signal. Immediately there was a rush. We had to cross a field, surmount a barbed wire fence, scramble through a ditch and then cross a road before reaching the comparative safety of the wood 100 yards away. Enemy planes were bombing our old HQ, and tanks continued to shell the area. Simultaneously, sniper fire carpeted the perimeter of the wood in which we were all now sheltering, and for a time we could do nothing but lie low and wait for the racket to stop.

Things at last began to quieten down, and with approaching darkness the sniping and our answering firing almost completely stopped. In the meantime, we had got to work organising a cookhouse and sleeping quarters in our new home, and were left in peace for the night.

In this new location hidden in the wood we still received a number of visitors with no credentials, but on returning from a visit to the now deserted Municipal Farm I gave orders that henceforth no one who entered was to be allowed to leave. Some four or five civilians subsequently turned up, and all were put under arrest and held under guard in one of the sheds. Whether this was straining my authority I did not debate; I could not afford to have enemies inside as well as at our gates.

Some of the detainees told us that two German tanks were based in the village of Marcq, as well as a body of snipers who were occupying a mill. I thought it would be good for morale to make a sortie, to try to engage both targets, and to find out at the same time more about what was happening in the world outside the farm. Volunteers were called for, and some 25 men came forward.

With some misgivings I left my new second-in-command in charge, I had postponed confronting him—and in company with a cheerful band of volunteers made our way towards the village with the intention when we reached it of splitting into two parties, one to search out the tanks, the other to attack the mill. But before we could divide, we encountered one of the tanks; it was stationed at the edge of the village facing us as we emerged from the wood and one of the crew was standing beside it looking in our direction.

We made immediately for cover behind a hedge, and thus concealed were able to proceed in one body into the outskirts of the village. We emerged on to the road on which the tank was standing but behind it, and so able to approach it from the rear. The crew-man was still looking towards the wood when, at a range of about 40 yards, I gave the order to open fire with two Bren guns and two Boyes anti-tank rifles. He was hit immediately, but managed to clamber back into the tank, which swung round and returned fire with its machine guns. After further exchanges during which we suffered no casualties, it passed briefly out of sight, then reappeared and came towards us again from the opposite direction. We resumed firing when the tank was about 40 yards away and it did not come any closer. I optimistically assumed that this was because the crew feared the damage our anti-tank rifles might cause, but although we directed our fire at the tracks of the vehicle, its most vulnerable point, it was without any apparent effect.

A few of us moved from the verge on to the road itself to try to obtain a better firing position, and soon I noticed that the fire from the tank was not reaching low enough to hit us. It became clear that the tank's machine guns could not be depressed enough to reach the ground at such close range.

From my new position I managed to hit the tracks and suspension areas of the tank several times, but again without any apparent effect. Then the Boyes jammed, probably from overheating; but the hits I managed to score may have been enough to scare the crew, because after about 20 minutes the tank withdrew.

As there was little more we could do, and a strong possibility that the tank crew would call up reinforcements, I gave the order to retire to another wood which had been agreed as a rendezvous point, and instructed the senior sergeant to lead the main party on across the open ground beyond the wood and back to our HQ. I said I would cover the retreat with the aid of a Bren gunner, one of the riflemen from the QVR's.

While the rifleman and I were providing cover, a German machine gun crew drove up in a motor-cycle combination, and began to set up a machine gun post only twenty yards or so from where we were lying. They did not see us, for we were hidden behind some bushes, but we could watch their movements without difficulty. Altogether six or seven soldiers made up the crew, and they set up the post very quickly, while despatch riders came and went ceaselessly; there was an atmosphere of bustle and efficiency about the whole operation.

Our men were all safely across the open field before the post was ready for action, however, and were concealed in the wood when the post commander appeared and began to study through binoculars the area surrounding our HQ.

There was now no way the rifleman and I could cross the field ourselves in daylight, so while we waited for nightfall we decided to make a cautious reconnaissance of the village in our vicinity, in the hope of finding shelter. Quite soon we came on a house in a side street of which the front door was open and went in. Two elderly people, obviously man and wife, disappeared down some stairs to a basement as we entered. I assured them that we would not harm them or do any damage, and that we would leave when it was dark, but they remained below. At dusk, as promised, we left and made our way back to the rendezvous point in the wood. There was no one there; we went on to the farm which we had left full of people in the morning. On arrival, we found to our amazement, that it was completely deserted.

The small equipment salvaged from the Ferme Municipale was still lying about, and our personal kits and bedding were still there, but practically everything else was gone. We assumed that under the threat of another attack my mysterious second-in-command had ordered the evacuation. My earlier doubts about him resurfaced with renewed intensity. I felt certain that he was an enemy agent, and that in my absence he had deliberately promoted an atmosphere of panic. In the face of a real or anticipated attack it would have been easy for him to order a withdrawal, and soon to have everyone rushing off helter-skelter to the beaches a mile or two away.

Whatever the explanation, panic just did not fit in with my view of the men in my unit, a good steady lot despite their lack of battle experience. I resolved I must locate them.

Early next day we made our way, unhindered to the coast, which seemed to be all that was open to us, and even that none too certain. Seven or eight miles east of Calais we contacted a body of some hundred or so men of the QVR and the Rifle Brigade, most of them lying about in a state of complete exhaustion, and my companion was happily reunited with his mates. I have always remembered his cheerfulness, courage and good sense with great respect and appreciation. He was, I remember, a joiner in civilian life.

Of my own unit I saw not a sign nor did anyone have any news of it. As I walked along the beach among the motley groups of exhausted troops of all ranks and many units, some wounded many without equipment, it came to me very forcibly that, at least for a while, our fighting days were over. The urgent thing now was to get away to regroup and re-equip.

But there was no way out behind that dismal beach, the only way was the sea, and out there, unbelievably, were British ships, as yet free from enemy attention.

I joined a small group, obviously like-mind, unsuccessfully attempting to signal those distant ships, and the senior officer, a major, told me that German tanks were expected at any moment, in the face of which, he said, there was no choice but to surrender, if we were even given that chance.

"No choice," I said, "except to swim for it."

He nodded a bit dubiously but made no comment.

My determination growing, I wandered off to where a sergeant-major and a corporal stood, in silence, gazing out to sea.

TWO

A Swim

"The sea," I said again, more to myself than to them. "It's all that's left to us now. It has to be the answer."

They were not impressed, but it wasn't their job to argue. One on either side of me, they squatted down on the damp sand and watched while I tugged at my heavy boots.

"That ship out there is our last sight of the Navy. It's bound to push off soon. It's not going to hang around outside Calais, now."

The sergeant-major looked his enquiry. The corporal stared stolidly at the ship. We had met up only five minutes ago.

"It's useless trying to signal them from this beach, but if I swim out I could get them to send a boat in under my direction, to gather up the stragglers."

22

I piled my kit on top of my boots, and was ready to go.

"You a good swimmer, sir? She's a mile or two out."

"Good enough. Mustn't hang about or we shall have their tank patrol down on us. Keep an eye on my boots."

Wearing only my waterproof watch and feeling extremely exposed I moved gingerly over the unattractive but near-empty beach, and then plunged in.

Considering it was late-May 1940, and the hottest summer for ages, the water seemed freezing cold. I turned for a last look at the beach, and with a wave to the sergeant now standing over my clothes, struck out seawards. I concentrated all my attention on the ship, which was at first difficult, as I was now much lower than I had been on shore, and the vessel was below my horizon. I had a rough sense of the direction, however, and swam on, snatching occasional glances back as some sort of guide to the angle of my course.

After a while I could no longer see the beach, only a silhouette of the higher ground surmounted by trees which lay behind it. Then the ship came fully into view, but incredibly it was as far as, if not farther than, when I set out.

I seemed to have entered an entirely other world, in which I was completely alone, the only sounds from the curl of foam as it broke round me, and my now laboured breathing. I began to feel as though I were in a cell without windows, and all I could do was to continue endlessly to swim on and on, reaching nowhere. The sense of isolation was overwhelming, not only physically but casting a huge shadow of doubt over my purpose.

I swam for what must have been an hour but seemed much more. Time and distance were now merged into an everlasting greyness. Suddenly, and very distinctly, there was a burst of gunfire from the shore, still behind me, and while I was vaguely speculating on this, there was a sharp snapping sound which drove me down, swimming under water for a few seconds. As I surfaced I expected to be met with bullets; I was convinced they had ricocheted off the surface in my vicinity.

Forced to take a new view of my surroundings I realised that the tide now had a relentless hold on me and that my objective was fast disappearing. I felt no reluctance at turning back towards the shore.

Swimming back was a dispiriting and gruesome experience. Thick black oil covered a huge area which I could not avoid and which threatened to drag me down. I knew my strength was failing and I began to wonder if I would ever make it. Only my tiredness stopped me from flailing around in a panic, and then I was suddenly stumbling along, crawling up the shingle, clear of the tide. I had the impression that the ship had changed its profile, making away from the coast. It no longer mattered. What did cause me concern was to find that the beach was now deserted. I made a stumbling course towards what I hoped was my kit but which turned out to be a heap of seaweed. Decidedly chilly now, I crouched down, still wary about the emptiness of the beach, and none too happy about my nakedness. It seemed desperately important to find my boots, and I was filled with indignation at the disappearance of their guardians.

Not only had my clothes gone, but with them were my identity papers. The full implications of this situation did not immediately sink in; a soldier without papers has no identity for friend or foe. What price, then, a naked one?

A more careful survey showed equipment of various kinds lying about and I seized an abandoned blanket with relief. Another hump revealed itself as a wounded and unconscious French soldier. There was nothing I could do for him, but I hoped that a German search party would soon come to his aid. That line of thought prompted me to leave the beach, picking up a battle-dress top which I quickly put on, feeling warmer but increasingly ridiculous, and making for the sand dunes above, and which I used to guide me in the direction of our reserve HQ in the woods.

Crouching among the tussocky dunes, I saw a patrol of German SS troops in navy-blue battle-dress, but without helmets or headgear, moving along in single file. There were about fifteen or twenty of them, young men carrying tommy guns, and clearly searching for Allied soldiers who had escaped capture. Two hours ago there had been a hundred or so men of the QVR and the Rifle Brigade, most of them lying about in a state of complete exhaustion, and I could only hope they had all got clear. I lay motionless until the patrol had moved out of sight, then very cautiously, but as fast as I could in my outlandish get-up, continued towards the wood.

Presently, in this unnaturally deserted landscape, I saw a small cottage, and driven on by my still shivering semi-nude state, I decided I must take a chance. If she felt any astonishment the kind, and brave, lady who came to the door did not show it. My chattering teeth did not too badly mar my reasonable French, and without any questions or comment she gave me a cup of coffee and an overcoat, and with a grave smile bade me 'Bon voyage'. For this spontaneous act of kindness she risked severe punishment, and I shall always be grateful to her. Fortunately I remembered in time to make a cautious survey of the quiet surroundings before slipping out into the lane.

Equally cautious was my reconnaissance on approaching my former HQ in the farmhouse which I had left only a few hours ago on our abortive sortie.

Incredibly, it was unoccupied and little damaged. I wasted no time in getting back into dry clothes and a properly fitting battle-dress, and in digging out for myself a good meal, noting with some self-satisfaction that we had made an excellent job of transferring our stores here from the now badly damaged Municipal Farm at Marcq.

I was so pleased to find myself recovering from my

tomfool-exploit that it took some time to register that I was completely alone.

Satisfied that the entrance gates were still effectively blocked I stretched out gratefully on my own camp-bed. Somewhere, with Calais a mere seven or eight miles away, ground was being contested as our troops withdrew towards the sea.

Hazily, as I sank into sleep, I said again to myself, "The sea. It must be the answer."

THREE

'Ci'

In the Army, as I had been at pains to learn, and to teach, you are never on your own; frequently a disagreeable fact, occasionally a comforting one. When I sat up, instantly fully awake, the realisation that I was quite alone hit me with an almost physical force. It was not in the manual, not this vacuum, no friends, no enemy. Momentarily my mind reverted to that eerily empty beach.

Prompted by an instinctive need for speed and silence, I dressed and found some food. More importantly, as it seemed, I found an admirable pair of boots which restored some feeling of normality, though they clattered too loudly in the seeming emptiness of the big room.

I checked myself from stepping too readily into the quiet yard, but there was no sound or movement there, and as I cautiously ventured further, back to the nearby Municipal Farm, there was nothing there to link it with yesterday's action; the buildings had suffered badly from further shelling and a fire was burning quietly as though tended, but there was no one in sight.

Undecided, still reconnoitring, I went on to the Calais–Dunkirk road, so recently choked by streams of refugees, and found it now completely deserted, except for some abandoned French army trucks, riddled with bullet and shell holes. Disinclined to expose myself too openly even in this deserted landscape I moved carefully along, finding them strangely empty. All except one.

Curled up in the drivers cab of the supply truck was a large, black Alsatian dog. He regarded me as suspiciously as I did him. I had never owned an Alsatian and I fully subscribed to the notion that they were unreliable in temperament and tenacious in attack. I made coaxing noises but his gaze remained steady and sceptical. But he and I were the only living creatures in this unreal landscape, and whatever his reputation, or because of it, I felt an urge to have him on my side.

He watched without a move as I went off to the farm, where I found two tins (large) of corned beef. Just as stubbornly he watched me open them, near enough for him to catch a whiff, as I gently murmured: "Ici". He stirred enough to give the beef a half-hearted look, but still did not rise. At last, getting impatient, I called peremptorily: "Ci!"

Without more ado he got up, looking much blacker and larger, jumped down from the cab and came meekly up to me. I gave him a pat on the head and put the meat in front of him, and with a wag of the tail he at once gave himself up to enjoying the meal. When he had finished I went back to the farmhouse and Ci followed, now without question my dog and clearly, in his opinion, officially on the strength of my unit. With Ci on hand I was certainly no longer a loner.

At once he became sentry, guard, companion and most

faithful of soldiers. His military training showed unmistak-
ably; discovering his capabilities was a joy, and a great boost
to my self-esteem as a French linguist as well. I began to test
him almost at once, taking him to the woods and commanding him in French—"Restez! Gardez!"—to look after a haversack. He remained by it for the rest of the day. But that night
he gave me a few bad moments, for he insisted on sharing
with me my small camp bed. It was barely big enough for
me, and I was determined not to let him get away with the
best half of it. So very firmly I pushed him off half a dozen
times. Equally firmly, each time he came back for more,
obviously regarding the proceedings as a game. Finally I
realised that only a violent physical confrontation would
convince him of my seriousness—and that could lead to
unknown consequences. He was, I reflected, a soldier, well
trained in man-assault . . . in short I gave up the struggle.
From then on, he slept like a child, stretched out by my side.
It was obviously the normal thing for him to do, a custom
for which I blamed his previous master; but I could not deny
that in other respects I was greatly in his previous master's
debt. Without analysing it I was aware of a change in my
outlook.

It had been uncomfortable and somehow irregular to be
in uniform, still free, but without orders or objective—no
combatative intention. But I now felt purposeful. If I could
not embark on a one-man offensive I could be positive in
evading capture, searching out with Ci how best to find and
join up with whatever active allied forces might still be in
the neighbourhood. Despite the evidence, I was not yet
prepared to accept that there were none.

The countryside seemed only lightly infested by the
enemy, and Ci and I soon discovered that it was comparatively easy to move about by night. The Germans' main
tactic in establishing control in those early days was to
create a state of terror, and thus keep everyone indoors.
Their numbers were in fact amazingly small; there were a

few tank crews, backed up by scattered bodies of snipers, and some SS units. Some of the snipers were SS men, others were undoubtedly local fifth columnists who earlier had sheltered the odd parachutist. The SS units, one of which I had seen from the sand dunes, were composed of raw-looking lads wearing navy blue battle dress and carrying Tommy guns. They looked as though they had been recruited straight from the Hitler Youth movement. Like the local population, the Germans seemed mostly to stay indoors after dark.

Ci's method of conducting night patrols was highly professional. On the command 'Allez', he would run ahead to the next likely checkpoint, a bridge, crossroads or whatever and there he would cast around with as much noise as possible, usually picking up something, a piece of wood or, on one occasion, an old boot and then playing with it dragging and throwing it around, as if he were still a puppy. Meanwhile I would wait behind to see if the racket flushed out a sentry. If there were no shots and no challenge, I would come forward and we would continue on to the next danger point. Although this procedure exposed Ci to constant danger, I felt sure that in the dark his lithe black body would easily elude the aim of any sentry he roused.

I went with Ci into the village of Marcq on two successive nights, and neither time did we encounter any German sentries. The most astonishing sight to meet our eyes was the spectacle of two tanks parked neatly one behind the other in a quiet residential side-street. We passed them safely, after Ci had carried out his usual skilled and noisy reconnaissance. I pictured the crews tucked up comfortably in bed for the night in one of the houses, their vehicles parked outside just like cars in peacetime, unwatched and unguarded. What I could do with a few Molotov cocktails or grenades, I thought.

On the third evening after Ci had joined me, I was taking the air after dark on the short road between the farmhouse and the entrance gate when I heard approaching footsteps, loud, clear and without any concealment. Only the enemy made the roads ring in that way, and I assumed without doubt that German soldiers were coming to the farm. I stepped back into the undergrowth which grew thickly along the side of the road, and as the marchers came up cocked my revolver and took aim in their general direction. Then, to my amazement a voice said in English "Who's there?" I emerged on to the road to find three British soldiers, two captains and one private (who turned out to be their batman) confronting me. They had heard the click of my revolver being cocked, recognised the sound, and realised at once that a German hearing them would not have hidden, but would immediately have called out to them to halt. They must have been under some special protection for I was ready to shoot at the very moment that one of them spoke.

We began to compare notes. It seemed that they had escaped from one of the forts in Calais and, travelling by night, were hoping to get to the forest of Guines, some eight miles to the south, where they planned to adopt a sort of Robin Hood existence. We soon realised we were all in the same boat, for I had no clear idea what to do next, and knew that it could only be a few days before I was winkled out of my present retreat. Any kind of concerted action was better than skulking aimlessly around, even in Ci's company. So when my new companions suggested that I join them in their bid for the forest I agreed without hesitation, meanwhile inviting them to make the farmhouse their home and to take any of the stores they wished.

They accepted my hospitality for the night, and next day we all prepared packs of provisions, planning to move on after dark. We were interrupted once by two enemy scout tanks which passed through the farmyard. They took us by surprise, coming from behind a barn round a bend in the farm road, and we only just had time to hide by diving into a haystack and covering ourselves with hay. As it was, we had an excellent view of them as they drove past, only five or six feet away. I was smoking a cigarette at the time and in the rush to find cover forgot to put it out, which in any case would have taken up time, and might have left a tell-tale wisp of smoke from the stub. So I found myself under a load of hay with a lighted cigarette in my hand, which I dared not extinguish for fear of attracting attention. I did not think that the tank crew were very likely to notice the trail of smoke it made, but there was the danger of the hay catching fire. I remained absolutely motionless, however, and the tanks continued on their way, without stopping or even slowing down; and within a few moments they were out of sight.

Immediately they were gone, one of the two captains turned on me and gave me a good dressing down for endangering everyone's safety. I pointed out that the tanks had appeared so suddenly that I had not had time to put my cigarette out; that if to do so I had delayed getting into the hay I might well have been seen, when everyone would have been even more endangered; and finally, that having got into the hay, any movement I made would have been more conspicuous than the cigarette smoke itself. The captain, however, did not appear to accept my explanation very favourably, and our relationship became somewhat cooler thereafter. For my part I began to doubt whether we would see eye to eye on other matters, particularly concerning Ci.

With the captain's reprimand ringing in my ears, I realised uneasily that I had, in fact, completely forgotten Ci, and that he might well have given us away if he had been seen by the tank crews. I looked round for him but could not see him anywhere. Anxiously I asked if anyone knew where he was. "Yes," said someone, "he's down here," and pointed to the hay at his feet. I called, and to my astonishment out crept Ci, wagging his tail, and came up to me and licked my face. Like the good soldier he was, he had completely effaced himself during the emergency.

That night, as soon as it was dark, we set out on our journey south towards the forest of Guines. There are numerous canals in the area east and southeast of Calais, and soon we encountered the first of an endless succession of bridges which we had to cross. Without Ci's aid we would never have been able to negotiate them successfully, but he led us unerringly over all of them, using to perfection the probing tactics he and I had practised previously. Because of this, I did not again forget him. The truth was that without him we should often have been completely lost and would have taken four or five nights to cover the distance that with his help we had achieved in one.

I was amazed, therefore, when someone, I think the captain who ticked me off, suddenly suggested that Ci was more nuisance than he was worth. He argued that if it became known that Ci was with us, he would give us away merely by being spotted. I felt incensed at this attack on my friend, the more so as I seemed to be in a minority; for the other captain, and their batman both expressed similar views. I was particularly annoyed that they all doubted Ci's ability to keep quiet in an emergency. I replied that he was a fully trained army dog, and could be totally relied on to keep quiet when necessary; and as to giving us away if he was seen, surely our uniforms would do that far more effectively than a dog! And I reminded them that when we had first encountered each other in the farm, Ci had not made a sound, whereas any ordinary guard dog would have created a terrific commotion. Anyway, nothing would make me leave him behind.

Although we had walked all night, in the morning we were still not far from Marcq, or Calais itself. In the early hours we found ourselves on a towpath beside a canal in a thickly populated area, with houses fronting the path as far as we could see. The district seemed to have been untouched by the war; there were no signs of damage or of enemy occupation, and barges were still moving along the canal. We had planned to hole up during the day, and the problem of where to do so began to become critical. There were very few people about, and as it grew lighter we decided to ask at one of the houses if we could shelter in it till the evening. None of us really wanted to knock someone up, but as the morning mist cleared, and people started to emerge we realised we had to find shelter fast. So we tried at one door—and got it slammed without a word in our faces. We tried at several more, but at each met with the same reception, and soon we were desperate. The local people, it seemed, were living in a world of total self-deception: there was no war, and people like us were uncouth undesirables, to be avoided at all costs.

Then suddenly, while we were still on the towpath, we came face to face with a German patrol, luckily for us on the opposite side of the canal. Time, I recall, stood still: I felt rather like a guilty schoolboy caught redhanded in some mischief. There was a guttural cry of "Halt", and as one, we dispersed, Ci and I jumping down the bank from the towpath on to lower ground where we were out of sight of the Germans.

After a little while our companions rejoined us, and, though I cannot recall exactly when or where, we had a hurried discussion about what we should do. The captain with whom I'd had words, and the private both decided to give themselves up. The other captain was, I think, initially uncertain about what course to follow, but finally stayed with Ci and me below the towpath.

I at once started running with Ci along the foot of the bank towards some open fields, and as soon as the captain realised where we were making for, he followed. There was no undergrowth or other cover and the surrounding countryside was flat and open; it was only because we were concealed from the enemy patrol by the banks of the canal,

in what militarily is called 'dead ground', that we were able
to make good our escape. There was a patch of trees about
200 yards away, and I thought that we could reach it before
the patrol could get across the canal, there being fortunately
no bridge in the vicinity. We went helter-skelter, hampered
by countless ditches and culverts which at first we did our
best to jump; soon however, we were wallowing up to our
knees in mud. Ci once again was a model of soldierly
conduct, keeping abreast of us with ease, not making a
sound, and striding along as calmly and confidently as if on
a training exercise.

Luckily we found a ditch heading directly towards the
trees, and scrambled along it until halted by a fence. Beyond
the fence we could see a paddock, which the trees sur-
rounded and screened, so we were able to climb into it
unseen, and having done so made our way across it
towards some farm buildings on the far side. There was a
yard in front of these, and to get into the courtyard from the
paddock was easy: we had only to climb a post and rail
fence. To get out on the other side, however, was another
matter: the exit was blocked by a high wooden plank fence,
flanked on each side by massive brick walls and by the
farmhouse itself. I had the impression as we climbed into
the place that I saw a door in the house closing, and remembering the response of local people to our requests for help
earlier, decided not to look for aid again. We raced on to the
fence, which was smooth and slippery, with only the barest
of handholds. Desperately I hoped that the impetus of my
approach would carry me up and over it.

Both the captain and I were feeling the effects of our long
run, following our all night walk, and neither of us had
much strength left. It was only with great difficulty that we
were able to hoist ourselves over, but we just managed it.
As usual I had left Ci to fend for himself, and it was a
dreadful shock to me to hear his anguished whimper from
the other side of the fence. I could not see him through the

close-fitting planks, and had to listen in horror as again and again he hurled himself at them in an attempt to follow us. It was to no avail, however; he could not reach the top, and slipped back every time to the ground. His yelps rose to a crescendo, and were followed by a succession of heart-breaking sobs.

"Leave him, and come on. Better without him," said the captain impatiently.

Hating him for that, and hating myself for accepting the inevitable, I plodded on and left Ci to his fate.

I had many excuses for abandoning him. I knew I could not climb back over the fence and then reclimb it carrying him; my companion in any case was already running on so I would have had no help from him. And the inhabitants of the farm seemed to be stirring. In the end it would have made little difference, for in a few hours we were captured, and there is no knowing what might then have happened to him. He would not have been a compliant captive. Yet over the years I have not completely lost a feeling of guilt that I abandoned Ci. I hope life dealt kindly with him.

We soon found a shed in which to hide. It was open on one side, and contained a row of about a dozen beehives facing the open side. Between the hives and the rear wall there was just room for us to crouch down out of sight of any passers-by. We were so exhausted that although we could not lie down, we were soon fast asleep.

In the early hours of the morning we were roused by shouts, and as we struggled into wakefulness, a German soldier appeared in front of us. Clearly he had been tipped off, by the local resident who hovered at his heels. He, however, had little time for his informant. He told him brusquely to shear off, but showed us the greatest courtesy. He held us under guard until a second soldier appeared, and then told us to get up and follow them. Encouraged by two rifles pointing at us, we did as we were told, though not before I had managed to secrete my revolver under one of the beehives; they would no doubt have confiscated it, anyway. We were taken to their unit's headquarters, which were in a substantial house in a nearby village, where one of the soldiers remained with us outside on guard while the other went in to report and obtain further orders. Unaccountably, our guard gave each of us a bar of chocolate, which seemed to me a good sign and cheered me up considerably. My companion, however, was full of foreboding, and said in a voice of doom that he was sure we were both going to be shot. After a long time, the soldier who had gone for orders came back down the steps of the house looking grim, and I began to fear the captain might be right: we both prepared ourselves for the worst.

We were put in a truck and driven some distance to the town of Desvres, where the football stadium had been converted into a prisoner-collection camp. Here we were delivered into the charge of guards somewhat more blasé than our first captors; they welcomed us by searching our packs and removing our wristwatches and other valuables, but leaving my money intact. The guards were changed at intervals, and at each change the new guards wanted to repeat the search; but I found that saying in German: "Ich bin schon 'mal gesucht'", (I have already been searched) effectively stopped them. Presently I found some survivors of my outlying detachments deployed on operational sites, and also of troop HQ personnel; they confirmed that they had been ordered to evacuate the farm and move to the coast by my mysterious second-in-command, reinforcing my conviction that he was indeed a fifth-columnist. I also found the colonel commanding our Regiment sitting in the stand in the front row alone. I reported to him briefly what had happened to my unit, after which I did not see him again.

After a few hours we were formed up in sections into a long column numbering perhaps a thousand. As we were being mustered, I encountered one of the other troop commanders from my battery, and he and I joined forces with four Royal Marine officers, our intention being to help each other in any way we could and to share out what possessions we had, including incidentally the bar of chocolate given to me when I was captured. Acting as a group proved well worthwhile, particularly in making the best of things during the overnight stops: from the beginning one member went ahead each evening to claim a good pitch for us. I don't know whose idea this was, but it certainly paid off, and I wondered whether it was a lesson learnt in the '14–18 war.

After a long wait, we were ordered to start marching and set off to the accompaniment of a great deal of shouting by the guards. Each section was preceded and followed by a lorry carrying a machine gun manned by three soldiers and the road was continually patrolled by both motor-cyclist and pedal-cyclist guards. No one knew where we were going, but the direction was east, and the general opinion was that we were almost certainly heading for Germany.

FOUR

Prisoner into Farmer

As we plodded slowly eastwards I had plenty of time in which to think. Food and shelter were outside our control, and already we were settling down to a take-it-as-it-comes Army routine. But for me, at least, it stopped there. I was far from resigned to being a prisoner of war, and the active part of my brain was wholly concerned with the idea of escape.

Our general direction was eastwards but we were still within reach of the French coast, and for me that was still the answer. Somewhere, preferably beyond the fighting zone, it must be possible to find a boat—some sort of boat—and get it across the Channel. Not that I knew much about boats, or seamanship, but at this stage that did not seem crucial. Later on, doubtless it would be, but first things first.

The urgent thing was to escape before getting to a POW camp. We had not heard much about them but it needed little imagination to envisage their general inaccessibility and stringent security. Germany was an impossible distance from the sea. The time to go was now.

As a prelude to escaping I thought I should test the reactions of the guards, and very soon, at a roadside rest, I wandered casually up an alley to a farmhouse. A woman, possibly the farmer's wife, stood in the broad doorway, watching me approach. I strode on. There was no sound from behind. Quite expressionless, as I came up to her, she reached into capacious pocket of her smock-overall, and held out an egg, which I accepted with alacrity. She was in the process of handing me a second one when a guard spotted me. I caught his movement over my shoulder and turned to face him. As matter-of-fact as the woman, he merely motioned me to get back to the main road, and he did this calmly, without any shouting or histrionics, both of which were frequent when there was any ordering to be done. And he showed no sign of using his gun, which encouraged me considerably. Here, I reckoned, was a comparatively simple method of getting away should a suitable moment offer. Not that I expected much to be offered; already I knew that it was entirely up to me to spot and seize the opportunity.

I did not dare look back in gratitude as we started moving again almost at once. I had in fact been able to take the second egg and counted them no small treasure. No good waiting for cooking facilities, so, remembering Tom Sawyer's method, I experimentally pierced a hole at each end and quickly sucked. I thought it was delicious and offered the other egg to my companion but he waved it away with distaste, apparently disapproving of such crudity. So I had it myself, and enjoyed it even more than the first. It was not too soon, I thought, to start living off the country.

At the end of the first day, we were locked up in a village church, where we made ourselves fairly comfortable in the pews. We were each given half a boiled potato for supper, brought round to us by a woman from the village; I think they had been freshly dug—at any rate mine tasted like ambrosia! Understandably, perhaps, I had failed to bring a mess-tin with me and so had to take my potato in my cupped hands. As it was firm and not too hot, this was no problem, but the next night I was not so lucky. We were halted in a field, and had to queue up at the entrance for our rations. Each man was given a ladle-full of what looked like quite good stew, but most of mine went straight through my hands, and I was glad to retain just some of the meat. Later, though, things were a little better. The majority of us had to spend the night lying in the field without shelter, but our little group's system of sending someone ahead paid handsome dividends, and secured us good places in the loft of a shed. The third night we reached Fresnes and were locked up in the prison. Although the conditions were better, the feeling of incarceration gave us all a taste of what it would be like when we reached our final destination. Our treatment seemed harsher too, and a roll-call was taken for the first time, our names being entered in a register.

On the fourth day of the march my feet started giving serious trouble; they had got soaked from running through the ditches away from the German patrol when we were taken prisoner, and afterwards I had completely overlooked the chore of drying them. Consequently, after four days of marching without taking my boots off, they had become swollen and so painful that when we stopped for rests I had to continue marking time to relieve the pain. I refused to dwell on the implications this might have for a man on the run. I realised that if I was going to make a break, action could not be long delayed; further, I knew that the convoy was nearing the point where its route north eastwards towards the German frontier would irrevocably diverge from the route back to the coast, which I needed to take. As we trudged slowly on, I never stopped looking for a chance to try out my escape ideas.

I was walking with considerable difficulty when we reached the little town of Boursies, a few miles short of Cambrai. My vigilance was rewarded as I realised that the road took a dog-leg turn as it entered the village, first to the right and then to the left. There were buildings on each side, and from my position towards the rear I saw that, after rounding the second bend, for a few seconds part of the column was completely out of sight of the guards, both the machine-gunners in the lorries, and the cyclist patrols. As I reached this crucial position, I noticed a pathway to the right of the road, an alley between two buildings. On the spur of the moment I slipped away from the column, and walked quietly but rapidly up the alley, being hidden in a few moments behind one of the buildings. As I went, some-one shouted in what seemed disastrously stentorian tones: ''What are you doing, Bill?'' Shuddering, I put a finger to my lips begging silence.

I stood stock-still, hunching my shoulders against the inevitable shout from the guards. My hiding-place behind a house seemed brazenly exposed as I peered through a small aperture and watched, incredulously, the tail-end of the column drag itself round the bend, out of sight, then out of sound. There was a moment of perfect silence.

I had escaped.

Suddenly, to my surprise, I was aware of a French civilian standing silently by my side, apparently watching as intently as I had been.

I had to restrain myself from clapping him on the back and shouting the incredible news to him, but instead I asked in my best French, a bit breathlessly, if it would be all right for me to continue along the path. Expressionlessly, he said it would be all right, certainly. With that he disappeared as unobtrusively as he had come, and I never saw him again.

It now seemed urgent for me to withdraw from the public gaze, though there was no sign of a living soul. About twenty yards ahead I saw a large barn backing on to the path, and, my sore heels disguising my haste, I was soon in its welcome shade. Opening a small door with some difficulty and caution, I managed to squeeze in, unobserved so far as I could ascertain.

The dim interior smelt comfortingly of hay, straw, and freedom. Deciding that I had had quite enough for one day I determined to bed down there and then for a good night's dreamless sleep. When I woke, stiff and thirsty, I sensed it was well past dawn. The sweet-smelling hay with which I had stuffed my boots seemed to have improved them immeasurably and I no longer shrunk from the thought of wearing them. I took a long time to put them on, lacing them with exaggerated care as I collected myself for my first day of freedom. The need for urgency, to run and keep on running, was still with me but over-ridden now by the absolute need for circumspection. I had got away, too easily perhaps, but the paramount objective was not to be caught again.

There was no sound from outside, muffled as it would be by the immense walls, and I had to make an effort to clamber down to the massive doors, to find out how I was situated. It was tempting to stay in this dim quiet sanctuary, but thirst, and curiosity, spurred me on.

I found that the main entrance to the barn was on the opposite side from that by which I had entered. I opened one of the double doors just enough to peep through, and found that the barn faced on to a farmyard, complete with dunghill in the middle, with farm buildings grouped all round it. There were cattle sheds, stables with a granary loft above reached by stone steps, rabbit and hen houses, and directly opposite my peep-hole, the farmhouse itself. The only visible sign of life was chickens wandering around pecking at grain spilling down the steps from the granary; but somewhere I could hear the sound of cows lowing and shifting in the straw. After standing motionless at the door for some ten minutes, and satisfying myself that there was no sign of human activity, I cautiously opened it far enough to pass through, and stepped out into the farmyard.

There was no reaction, so then, very silently, I explored the yard, finding the cows tied up in stalls, and some tame rabbits in a hutch. I released the rabbits, finishing my tour at the back door of the farmhouse, which proved to be unlocked. I opened it cautiously, and found myself looking into the farm kitchen. Before going further, I went outside again to check if there were any other doors and to find, if I could, the location of the front door. There was no other entrance to the house from the farmyard; and I could not walk right round the outside of the house because the high walls which edged the yard were joined directly to it at each side. So I contented myself with looking into the house through the windows that opened on to the yard, to make sure as far as was possible that it was not occupied.

Satisfied on this point, I re-entered the house through the kitchen and found the front door opened direct on to a road. Then I made a thorough examination of the kitchen and larder, noting with satisfaction that the contents of the larder included a whole sack of rice. Strangely emboldened, I went on to search through the rest of the house. The stout stairs made no sounds as I went cautiously up to a well-lit landing. The first door was ajar and gave to my touch with the merest creak. The room was unoccupied.

I had all along decided that a change of clothing was my first need. To my delight, I found in a chest a typical farmer's outfit, corduroy trousers, cotton shirt and jersey. Quickly I bundled them under my arm and hurried back to the barn. They all fitted me reasonably well and I changed without delay. I hid my uniform under some bales of straw in a corner of the barn, but kept my army boots which seemed to fit my new identity, being well-coated with mud, and far from soldierly in appearance. A final touch I thought wise was to shave off my moustache, which I did without delay. With these outward changes completed I found that I had no difficulty in adapting to my new role.

Still with half an eye alert for intruders on my strange retreat, I began to explore. There were plenty of eggs in the henhouse, and some four or five cows, obviously even to my ignorant eye in need of milking, were tied up in the cow-shed. So I decided to organise myself a milk supply. This, however, proved not quite so straightforward a job as I had expected. I had often watched cows being milked, and thought there was really nothing much to it; but soon I revised my ideas. At first all went well; but each time I managed to get a bucket about a quarter full, the cow smartly took one pace forward and knocked it over. It took me six attempts to get half a bucket full; but a drink of the fresh milk quickly restored me, and without further delay I lit the wood-burning stove in the kitchen, and put some water on to heat. Meanwhile I examined the larder in more detail, hoping I might find butter and cheese, and possibly even wine.

Suddenly I was interrupted by the sound of a motor-cycle approaching, too fast and already too close, I thought, for comfort. I made a dash for the safety of the barn, thinking to escape if necessary, by way of the rear door and the path along which I had arrived the previous day. From inside the barn I saw a Germany army motor-cycle combination, one man driving and another in the sidecar, enter the yard through a gate in one corner which, inexplicably, I had previously overlooked. A search patrol already? And coming straight to my hide out!

But I was no escaping POW. I was now one of the locals and had better try out my part. With a straw in my mouth, I ambled with what I hoped was peasant unconcern to the

45

barn door. As soon as the two Germans saw me, they dismounted, and approaching, saluted and politely asked, in French, if I was the 'patron', the owner of the farm. I replied, also of course in French, I was his son, which seemed to satisfy them, for they then enquired if I had any eggs to sell. I replied that I had, and they immediately offered cigarettes and tobacco. Leaving the rate of exchange to them I took what they offered and they left, apparently well pleased with the results of their visit—as indeed I was myself. It occurred to me after they had gone that the Germans might already have visited the farm, discovered it was deserted, and helped themselves to eggs and anything else they could find. If so, they must have had quite a shock themselves when I appeared at the barn door. Be that as it may, they continued thereafter to call every day to exchange eggs for tobacco, and never questioned my status.

My first brush with the enemy in my new role as a civilian left me feeling well pleased for it showed that, on a superficial encounter I could easily pass as a Frenchman. Considerably relieved I returned to the house, and leaving the larder, explored the rest of it more thoroughly than on my first survey. I was delighted to find in one of the upstairs rooms a luxurious double bed ready made up, with spotless bed linen and covers. Returning to the groundfloor, I finished checking the larder, but sadly found nothing more of much interest there. A bottle containing a yellow liquid which I thought might be wine turned out to be cooking oil, and this I decided might be useful for anointing my swollen feet. Some treatment for them was my next priority, and after preparing a meal of boiled eggs and milky rice pudding, which I much enjoyed, I got down to a detailed examination of the damage to my feet. They were in a terrible condition, swollen red, and raw where the blisters had broken, and the pain, which after my overnight rest had subsided somewhat, had returned now more sharply than before. So I bathed them in warm water, and after-wards rubbed in some of the oil; and to my relief it eased them almost at once.

That night, after a dreamy day with no further inter-ruptions to my Crusoe-like solitude, I slept in the big double bed. I was not convinced that this was either entirely proper or prudent, but it was wonderfully comfortable. In the early hours of the morning, however, I was awakened by the sound of heavy feet tramping about downstairs. Checking my impulse to duck beneath the clothes, I lay still, waiting to see what would happen. An intruder or the owner? I was unprepared for either, and held my breath as the stairs creaked. Dimly I saw an unmistakable German uniform in the doorway, and at the same moment the man in it saw me. He stopped in his tracks, looked closely at the pile of clothing I had left by the bedside and which was patently civilian; then apparently satisfied, he turned without a word, and left the house at once. I realised that, in my new-found confidence I had foolishly omitted to check whether the front door of the farm was locked. Consider-ably chastened, I rectified the omission immediately, although I spent a far from restful night. In the morning light the episode seemed too bizarre to be taken seriously; who or what was he expecting to find? I half wished I had challenged him.

Later that morning I had another visitor; a lady who, it seemed, lived with her two daughters aged about 11 and 12, in a small cottage across the street from the farm. She came through the yard with the two girls, and knocked at the kitchen door. When I answered, she explained that she had been looking after the cows since the owner left about a week ago, and asked whether she should continue to do so. I replied unthinkingly that I was quite capable of caring for them and milking them; only afterwards did it occur to me that she might have been employed by the farmer, and that it would have been prudent to ask what her connection with him was. However she did not seem at all suspicious of me, nor asked what authority I had to be in the place. For my part, I was anxious to give her the impression that I had a right to be there, but I did not want to antagonise her. So I assured her she could continue to have a share of the milk and promised to keep some for her every day. This seemed to be what she wanted; she said she would either come over for it herself or send one of her daughters. Then she formally presented both the girls to me, at the same time asking them if they would be willing to fetch the milk for her. Both replied eagerly that they would.

She went on to say that she had been in the habit of entering the farm through the front door, and for this reason had left it unlocked; this morning, however, she had come into the yard through an entrance a little way down the street, and would be quite happy always to do so in future, as she could understand that I would want to keep the front door closed. Her daughters, she said, would come that way too when they came for the milk: I could give them messages if I needed anything. I thanked her and told her that I had already found a German soldier going through the rooms that morning.

At this point, I decided to give her a reason for my presence: I said that I was looking after the farm on behalf of the owner (luckily I had found his name on some papers), and she appeared to accept this explanation. At any rate she made no comment, although what her private thoughts were I could not tell.

My visitor then proceeded to explain in detail how she went about feeding and watering the beasts. Watering, it seemed, was the worst job, since it meant filling numerous buckets from a tap in the yard and carrying them to the trough in the cowshed. Then she referred to the problem of the bull, of whose existence I had been blissfully unaware. It was in a separate stall, she said, but should be put out daily to pasture. She left me to make what I liked of that; I remained inscrutable, but could not imagine for one moment handling the bull on my own. In fact I did not attempt to release it, but fed it regularly as I did the cows.

We continued to talk, and my visitor gave me several pieces of helpful advice: she told me which part of the hay to use first (I was surprised to learn that it mattered, it had all seemed the same to me). She advised me also about the grain for the chickens. This, as I had already seen, was spilling freely down the steps from the granary, and the chickens were happily helping themselves. However, I nodded appreciatively, and thanked her for her help. Finally she and her daughters prepared to leave. Before she did so I said that she must take her day's milk with her, which pleased her very much. We parted on good terms, which I resolved to maintain during my stay, the duration of which I could not foretell. I was glad to have someone to turn to for advice or information. When, a little later, I had the good fortune to discover a large sack of sugar, which was in extremely short supply, I was able to give these good neighbours some of it and this further improved our relations.

The next day the good lady, whose name I never discovered, came over to tell me that some English soldiers had called on her and asked for help; she thought I might like to see them. Clearly, although she had asked no questions and I had not told her anything about myself or where I came from, she had guessed that I was English. It seemed quite natural for me to trust her implicitly, and without hesitation I said I would like to meet these Englishmen, whereupon she disappeared and almost immediately returned with three British tommies, all in uniform. This caused me considerable alarm, for if the Germans had seen them coming into the farm we should all be in serious trouble. I decided therefore not to let on that I was English (an idea which did not seem to occur to any of them) and I addressed them in French. One of them asked me, also in

French, if I could tell him where the road outside the farm led. I gave a rather garbled reply, for of course, I did not know, and then asked him where he and his companions wanted to go. He turned to them and said, in English, "He wants to know where we are going. Shall we tell him?" to which they answered emphatically, "No". After that the conversation fell a bit flat. As my friend from over the way remained with us, it was impossible for me to speak openly, but there was in any case really nothing I could do to help them, apart from giving them a drink of milk and a few eggs, and I made no attempt therefore to persuade them to stay. Soon they went on their way, to my great but slightly guilty feeling of relief.

My main immediate concern was my feet, and I spent the day resting, and at frequent intervals rubbing them with the cooking oil. It seemed to have a good effect and after twenty-four hours they were sufficiently recovered to enable me to go out for the first time. The German soldiers who came to the farm for their eggs told me that they were camped quite near, and when I suggested that in future I bring the eggs to them they at once agreed. I thought it a good idea to see their set-up and so when I finally went out I decided to make their camp my first call.

I found it in a field only a short distance from the farm. My call appeared to cause no surprise: it seemed to be regarded as quite normal. For my part, I was amazed that entry was so easy. I saw no guard or evidence of security precautions during any of my visits. I was allowed to walk straight to the first tent inside the encampment, where a senior NCO was sitting with three lower ranks, engaged in what seemed a serious discussion. As I approached they broke off their discussion, looking at me questioningly, and I held out my bucket of eggs with one hand and pointed at it with the other. The chief NCO frowned, but he at the same time nodded and said something in an undertone to one of his juniors, who got up at once and went into the tent. He emerged again almost immediately with several packets of cigarettes, which he handed to me without a word, simultaneously taking the eggs. Picking up the empty bucket I then turned and walked away. The whole transaction, during which I did not speak a word, took only a few minutes. As I left I saw a number of heavy guns concealed under some trees and several lorries parked apparently at random.

I returned to the farm well pleased with what I had learned, and confident that the Germans were not interested in me and that I could safely explore the rest of the village. If the Germans were not interested, the local French population appeared non-existent; on my first sally I saw no sign of anyone except my neighbours across the road. So I decided to investigate thoroughly the houses in the immediate vicinity of the farm, and was soon embarked on a programme of wholesale pillage, which I assured myself was fully justified under the circumstances of war, notwithstanding my present non-participation.

My first major find was the sack of sugar; this was in an upstairs room in one of the largest houses in the village, which, judging by its furnishings and the quantities of food stored everywhere must have belonged to one of the leading residents. I filled a small bag with sugar on my first visit, and decided to get some means of transporting the whole sack to the farm in due course, but in fact I never did so. None of the houses I entered showed any signs of present occupation, although I suspected people were somewhere about. I felt sure, for instance, that the man I had seen in the alley when I first escaped must be still in the neighbourhood.

One of my most rewarding visits was to a small handyman's workshop where I found some very useful tools, including a pair of pliers and a pair of miniature wire-cutters of a type I had not seen before. The wire-cutters were invaluable in my subsequent house-breaking forays, for they could cut through steel rods up to a quarter-of-an-inch thick, and even hardened steel such as is used for padlock hasps. My booty from the workshop also included some small files, a screwdriver, a bradawl, several knives, matches and a torch. From another raid I acquired a cut-throat razor complete with strop, a great relief as my supply of safety razor blades was exhausted and I could find no replacements.

Oddly enough, in these nefarious forays the only person I encountered directly was another British soldier similarly engaged. After a little initial hesitation we spent a couple of hours together discussing our prospects. He was in uniform, and I told him he didn't stand a chance of escaping unless he changed into mufti (civilian clothes). He pointed out that a soldier caught thus was likely to be shot as a spy. It was either that, I said, or giving up the attempt to escape. I had some experience, I added, for when I was taken prisoner I was still in uniform, although trying to evade capture. We talked for a long time, and finally agreed to go our separate ways. Quite apart from this question of wearing uniform I came to the conclusion that I would be better off on my own; one slightly English looking civilian might pass muster, I thought, two together would be at once suspect. And there was another thing: if an emergency arose, two people together would need to discuss what to do, and if overheard this in itself would give them away. We parted with mutual doubts, but heartened at meeting one another.

All in all, during my stay in Boursies I underwent a valuable training course in breaking and entering; my schooling was of course made relatively easy because many of the houses were not securely closed. Often indeed they had been left completely open and unprotected. Not surprisingly, no money or valuables had been left behind by the occupants despite the haste of their departure. I found only one small trinket, a ring, fashioned I guessed by a small-time craftsman out of strands of copper wire with a sort of rosette on the front. I admired then the skill with which it had been made, and admire it still today. I bring it out sometimes to polish it, and as I do I seem to relive some of the adventures I had while I was on the run. It was the only thing I took which I did not need for my survival.

Sometimes, greatly daring, I ventured out of the village along the main road, keeping well out of sight of any passing traffic. German despatch riders frequently hurtled past, seemingly careless of possible danger from a hostile population. I considered the idea of stretching a trip wire across the road to stop one, then donning the rider's uniform, and taking off on his motor-bike. It was a crazy idea, of course, but an intriguing one to conjure with—and incidentally evidence of my increasing self-confidence which was, of course, founded on my ability to cope with the French and German languages, in both of which I was experienced to reasonable commercial standards. Without this, I doubt if I should ever have started.

A much more practical proposition was to acquire a pedal cycle, and I searched Boursies from end to end without success, apart from one or two wrecks. It was, in fact, partly because of this that I began to explore further afield. At last I came across one propped against the wall of an isolated farmhouse about a mile away from the village. I mounted it and rode off without hesitation. The farm seemed to be occupied, and I felt extremely ashamed of my barefaced theft; but without a bicycle I could see no way of getting to the coast.

The bicycle enabled me to explore a considerably greater area. I used only minor roads, and always took great pains to avoid being seen by the Germans. I was not always successful; once a despatch rider stopped when he saw me to ask the way. After a while I hit on the idea of carrying over my shoulder a hoe which I found in the farmyard, it would, I thought, be a convincing cover if I was interrogated.

During one of my expeditions I visited Hermies, quite a large village and the nearest place to Boursies. In several of the farms round about there was evidence that life was continuing normally, so I took still greater care than at Boursies to avoid being questioned, checking each farm I arrived at to make sure it was unoccupied before entering. My main preoccupation was to secure provisions for my journey to the coast, and I also urgently needed a map of the district. I did not come across much food, but found a very useful map incorporated in a post office almanac hanging on a kitchen wall.

At one small farm I noticed as I entered that the midden, established as usual in the middle of the yard, was steaming with what looked like freshly dumped manure. With this indication that the farm was probably being worked it was no place for me, and I was about to turn and quit the place when the back door of the farmhouse opened, and a pleasant, quite handsome woman dressed in working clothes came out. She asked what I wanted, and I said (I had the answer ready) that I was looking for a drink of water. She smiled and asked if I would not prefer a glass of beer. This struck me as an excellent idea and I replied "Yes" without hesitation. Soon I was sitting at the table in the lady's kitchen chatting with her over my drink. She asked me where I was going, and I told her that I was from the Belgian border area, and that I was looking for my family. I explained that I had been away from home at the time of the German invasion, and in my absence they had joined the stream of refugees going south; I had heard that a group of them had recently come this way and I was hoping I might catch up with them.

The lady told me that her husband had been called up to the French army, and was now reported missing, and that she was looking for help on the farm, labour being very hard to find. Then she offered me a job. I was anxious to get ahead with preparations for my journey, and was therefore

54

very wary of getting into an entanglement; so I replied that
if I was successful in finding my family reasonably soon, I
would come back and discuss the idea further with her; but I
must find them first. Then, with a certain regret, I left her
and rode back to Boursies.

That evening I decided that I had probably exhausted the
possibilities of useful pillage in the area and that despite this
offer of employment, it was time to move on. I was more
than ever convinced that a boat offered the best, or indeed
the only chance of getting home, so I prepared for a journey
to the coast. I cooked six rice puddings, with two boiled
eggs in each, carefully wrapped them in greaseproof paper,
then packed them three at a time in cardboard boxes. I had
no bread, for there was nowhere in the village to buy any.
No doubt I could have got some in one of the still-occupied
farms, but I did not want to draw attention to myself, and in
any case was quite happy to live off rice puddings as long as
they lasted.

In the morning I filled my army pack, now looking a bit
nondescript, and fixed it behind the saddle of my stolen
bicycle: there was a carrier over the rear wheel, and on this I
secured another bundle containing spare clothing and
oddments. In addition, I also had a haversack, which I
planned to carry in the normal way, slung over one
shoulder, while riding.

I said goodbye to my neighbour, who tactfully refrained
from questions, and told her exactly where the sack of sugar
was. So, after nine days of living the life of a farmer, I
left my hide-out in this strange little oasis. As I headed
southwest I passed my erstwhile neighbour trundling the
sack of sugar on a wheelbarrow along the footpath. It was
a pleasant picture to take with me. I had not realised
how important the sugar had been in establishing a bond
with her until I saw the determination with which she
struggled to get it home. As for the Germans, the eggs
would be theirs for the finding, and I was confident that

they were unlikely to enquire into my non-appearance.

I headed southwest because I reckoned the chances of finding a boat close at hand between Calais and Le Havre would be slight, I rated Brittany a better proposition than Normandy, but I was sure that near the fighting there would be the danger of running into checkpoints at the major rivers which I would have to cross if I headed west. I therefore thought it advisable to go inland from the Calais area for at least 30 miles before turning west towards my ultimate objective. It was fine to be on the move again, whatever the hazards. I have had enough of my soft bed.

FIVE

'ZGRRH—GRTSCH—ACHRTS'

It was with considerable trepidation that I set out, wondering what might happen as I drew nearer to the German advanced units. I decided at first to keep to side roads to reduce the chances of confrontation with the enemy—for as such, and not as occupying forces I still regarded the Germans. Using the sun for navigation, I rode southwest; this I reckoned would take me towards the Atlantic coast, either in Normandy or Brittany. Not surprisingly, I found progress frustratingly slow; the roads were so winding that I soon lost all sense of direction, and began to suspect that I had done a U turn and was retracing my route.

After an hour or so I ran out of patience, and although I was scared at the thought of riding along main roads full of German convoys with the probability of road checks at frequent intervals, I decided that risks had to be taken if progress was to be made. Accordingly, at the next cross-roads I turned onto a major road—and at once saw a German convoy disappearing in the distance ahead of me. I decided to keep a low profile, merge into the background and make myself as inconspicuous as possible. My horror at what happened next may therefore be well imagined.

The roar of a motorbike suddenly burst into my con-sciousness and almost at the same time I heard a fierce, guttural shout. It sounded something like 'ZGRRH—GRTSCH—ACHRTS!' A German despatch rider flashed past, turning as he did so to look at me with teeth bared and an expression of blood-curdling fury on his face. I was petrified, and for several seconds continued mechanically pedalling, my brain numb with fright. Like a mesmerised rabbit I waited for the rider to return; but to my amazement he continued on his way without even slowing. As my brain came unstuck, I started to wonder what it had all been about; perhaps, I thought, it was an example of German terror tactics. Suddenly light dawned. I was riding on the wrong side of the road and what the German had shouted at me was, "Zur Rechts!" (Keep to the Right!) Promptly, if a little belatedly, I moved over to the other side of the road, thankful that it had not occurred to the despatch rider that he was passing an idiot Englishman who had forgotten where he was.

My self-confidence soon returned, and indeed I no longer sought to avoid these passing encounters with the enemy. Once on the main road I was in fact constantly overtaken by German traffic of every description, from heavy petrol tankers and light half-tracked personnel carriers to open command cars; but no one showed any interest in me. Presently I overtook a convoy of horse-drawn vehicles, complete with mobile field kitchens, which looked as if it had stepped straight out of the Franco-Prussian war of 1870; and I was then myself overtaken by a straggling body of

58

soldiers on bicycles of all shapes and sizes, obviously, like mine, appropriated en route.

As he overtook me, one of the German cyclist stopped, and grabbing the handlebars of my bicycle, roughly demanded we exchange machines. I objected vigorously, and a noisy argument developed, punctuated by comments from other soldiers as they passed. Some two or three dismounted and gathered round to give moral support to their man, who launched into an impassioned account of the length and difficulty of the journey he had to undertake. It was only right, he declared, that he should have my machine which was so much better than his.

One look at the broken-down contraption he wanted to palm off on me was enough to make me desperate: sensing that I was losing ground, I mounted a counter-attack, and equally passionately shouted my indignation at the unfairness of his demands. Encouraged by the quiet reception of my outburst, I became even more vehement and began to wave my arms and threaten all in sight with the wrath of my father. My father, I yelled in French, was 'le Maire' at the next village and a man of importance. I guessed that the soldiers, who for their part spoke only in German, would not understand much of what I was saying. One of them, however, turned out to be something of a linguist, and did some halting translation for both parties.

When I said my father was in the next village, I was immediately asked—"Wo? Où?", and realising that I was being taken seriously, I gave the name of the next village, which fortunately I had just seen on a signpost. For good measure, I added a final shot: "It's the very next village. We'll be there in no time, and then you will all soon be sorry!"

There was no response to this, and realising that I now had the advantage I developed my theme assiduously, threatening that I would see that my father informed the German Kommandant officially that they had tried to steal my bicycle by force; and that would be the worse for them.

Everyone remained silent, seemingly cowed by my eloquence; and thus encouraged I went on to new flights of rhetoric.

I have always been a slow speaker but now I knew that if I was to clinch victory I had to talk fast. So, I went on to picture in dramatic terms the fury of my father when he learnt how I had been tormented and misused and how my bicycle, a present on my last birthday, had been stolen. Followed a description of the long and arduous journey I had made from the north after visiting my aunt, and the trials and tribulations I had endured in travelling through the war-devastated areas; now, after so much suffering, I was at the end of my strength, I said, adding that it was all unfair, I just could not take any more. I shook my fist in a final frenzy and shouted that I would not spare a single soul who had wronged me. My father would demand the harshest punishment for them all, I roared, and then added, very deliberately, "Anyone I point out as having taken part in my mistreatment will be reported and taken immediately to the German Kommandant".

I could not tell how much the German soldiers understood of what I had said; it was probably very little, for I had given their interpreter no chance to keep up with me. In fact he had given up trying, and when I paused for breath I found he had disappeared. The rest of the soldiers had clearly lost heart; their attempt to take my bicycle petered out, and I decided to go for the *coup de grâce*. I began to hurl insults at them, feeling quite safe, since without the interpreter, I knew they could not understand me, and as a crowning shot shouted in execrable French, even as they started to back away, a phrase recalled from the French class at school: "Et mettez tous ça dans votre pipe et fumez ça!"—"Put that in your pipe and smoke it". There was no reply. Like dogs outfaced by a kitten, the soldiers drifted away.

A surge of relief and elation swept through me; I found I

was quivering with excitement and relieved tension, and I sat down as they passed meekly as a flock of lambs, giving them plenty of time to get clear. Nor did I then hurry to catch up with them again, being particularly anxious that they should clear the next village before I reached it!

A little after this, I found a complete wireless communication station, apparently of French origin, set up in the open air by the side of a farmhouse. Tables and chairs, obviously taken from the house, were arranged in a circle round the transmitter, which was mounted on what looked like a carrying case. The equipment looked as if it had never been used; presumably the intending operators had left in rather a hurry. I thought, however, that they might have left booby-traps, and presumably the Germans thought so too, for clearly they had left everything severely alone. I did not investigate too closely, and continued on my way after a brief look from a respectful distance.

Later the same day, near Bapaume, I came across the remains of the equipment of a Scottish unit complete with spare kilts; this I investigated without hesitation, not because of my confidence in the sporting behaviour of the Scots, but because everything was in such disorder that I was sure someone else had already been through it. I discovered that the unit had formed part of the 51st Highland Division, and that it must have been under attack shortly before I arrived.[1] My prizes were a kilt which I thought might come in useful as a blanket; and some Gervais cheese which I found nearby in an abandoned lorry in the form of a consignment of packets. I sat down at once, for it was past lunch time, and made a very enjoyable meal. I remember the taste of that Gervais with pleasure to this day. In fact, I ate more than I should have done, but happily suffered no ill effects. I also packed as much of it as I could into my

---

[1] I learnt afterwards that the unit reached the port of St Valéry-en-Caux, but that attempts there by the Royal Navy and Merchant Navy to embark the troops were foiled by fog, and that nearly all were taken prisoner.

haversack, and it brightened up my diet for quite a few days after.

Many houses were still deserted in the part of the country I had now reached, for the Germans had overrun it only in the last few days. Most of the inhabitants had abandoned their homes before the enemy arrived, leaving nearly everything intact, so I had no difficulty in finding first-class accommodation that night, finally electing to sleep in what was almost a manor house, which I came on just after passing through Peronne. It was set back from the road in its own grounds, and approached by an imposing drive. I had no difficulty in getting in—I think the front door had been purposely left open. This was often the case, I found; presumably it was done to avoid the damage caused by the door being forced.

The house appeared to belong to a Paris family; it was beautifully furnished and the bed I selected proved entirely satisfactory. There was a spacious and attractive library, which I went through with great interest, hoping to find a road map of the area towards Normandy and Brittany. Fortune smiled on me and I discovered a pocket Michelin guide which was just what I wanted.

There were a number of outbuildings which I investigated. I found they contained gardening implements and stores of various kinds, but in one there was something else: a silk parachute of German make. It had been left draped unfolded over the contents of a shed, and looked as if it had been thrown there in a hurry. Whether it had been left by a friend of the family, or by a German parachutist (who might indeed also have been a friend) I could not tell, but it provided me with material for several useful handkerchiefs.

Next day I set off after an excellent night, much more confident now that I had the Michelin to help me on my way. Indeed with the clearer appreciation of the geography of the area which Michelin had given me, I realised that the point where by chance I had left the prisoner column had in fact been an ideal one for my purpose. Boursies was the very place to which I should have headed if I had escaped earlier, before turning southwest. More by luck than judgement so far I had come the right way.

I had planned to cross the Seine about halfway between Paris and Rouen; and according to Michelin, Vernon looked the best point. I realised now, however, that travelling in that direction I should be following close behind the German advance, and if I caught up with it I might run into the fighting. There seemed a reasonable chance, however, that the Germans were advancing at least as fast as I was, and if this were so my fears would be groundless. What though if the French rallied at some point and held up the Germans even for only a short time? In that case I should be in deep trouble. So before starting I debated whether perhaps I should change my direction while I had a choice; but finally I concluded that the best course would be to carry on as intended, and to try to find out what was really happening before making any changes in the plan.

I passed through Montdidier and Beauvais without incident, though at Beauvais I saw an unusual spectacle: German soldiers ransacking a camera shop. Normally discipline among the German troops was strict and their behaviour very correct. I wondered if I was entering an advanced area where the regulations had not yet been enforced, or whether, perhaps, front line troops had greater licence than the back-up units to take booty from freshly conquered territory. The town in which there were many bombed and shelled buildings, certainly looked as if it had been attacked only within the last few days. Perhaps, I thought, I was already reaching the front.

SIX

A Schweinisch Encounter

Shortly after leaving Beauvais I arrived at a pleasant little village with a neat green in the centre of which was a crossroads. On the green the horse-drawn vehicles and gun limbers of a German field artillery unit were drawn up in tidy ranks, while near the crossroads in the shade of a tree three or four officers sat studying maps at small tables, which looked as if they had been taken from nearby houses; a short distance away their drivers waited by their staff cars. All around was bustle and activity, indicating to a humble farm labourer (which is what I hoped I looked like) that the Germans had only just arrived.

As I cycled past, the officers looked up and one or two of them seemed to me to give me rather searching looks. However, I passed without challenge, and on reaching the outskirts of the village was congratulating myself on having passed another hazard safely, when I saw the German equivalent of a jeep coming along the road towards me. As it passed, one of the occupants, a fat redfaced officer gave me a benign smile, to which for some reason I responded only with a blank stare. Perhaps it was because I thought there was little cause to worry about him, or perhaps because I felt subconsciously that such smiles were merely a method of ingratiation—totally insincere.

Whatever the reason for my cool response, my musings were rudely interrupted shortly afterwards by a jeep which approached from the village and stopped immediately it passed me, the driver getting out and waiting for me to reach him. It was not the jeep I had seen before, and the redfaced officer was not in it, but I felt sure that he had something to do with its appearance.

"Hier aufsteigen," (Get up in here) shouted the driver as I drew near, signalling to me to board the truck. I replied, in my role as a local farm worker, "Oui, M'sieur. Et mon velo?" (Yes, Sir. And my bike?)

"Lassen dort. Schnell. Schnell!" (Leave it there. Quick!), was the reply, the driver pointing to the ditch at the side of the road. Fearing that if I left my bicycle exposed, I might never see it again, I looked round for somewhere to hide it and the driver understandingly pointed to where the ditch was covered with bushes.

"Ja. Ja. Besser so," (Yes. Yes. Better there) he nodded, and waited while I hid the bicycle as well as I could.

Then I climbed up into the jeep beside him and without a further word was driven back to the village I had just left. As we went I tried to imagine the state of mind of an officer in the German army, such as the redfaced smiler I had just seen, as he was being driven through a conquered land. Having, I hoped, induced in myself the right frame of mind I ventured to ask in French a question which was understandably worrying me; where was I being taken?

"Nach d'm Dorf. Sie werden sehen," (To the village. You'll see) was the brief reply. I felt this was unhelpful and pressed a further question: would I be brought back soon? This produced no answer, so, hoping to improve relations, I switched to German and at once detected a better atmosphere.

"Ja. Ja. Was zu tun und dann bald zurückkommen" (Yes. Yes. Something to do and then soon come back). This was more reassuring, but my misgivings remained. Had the officers who saw me ride through the village penetrated my disguise? Had the redfaced one told them of my unsmiling response to his greeting, and was I to be punished for dumb insolence? I could only surmise, and before I had time to do much of that, the jeep reached the village green, where the officers were still poring over their maps. They looked up as it arrived, and I half thought that I detected a look of secret satisfaction on their faces as they saw me.

We drove right on to the green before stopping, the driver exchanging shouted comments with his compatriots the while. I could not understand what was being said, except for the one word 'Schwein', which I dismally noted cropped up several times. Presently the driver disappeared for awhile, leaving me in the jeep. When he returned he was accompanied by a young officer, who told me, mainly by sign language to get into the back; I did so, and then a soldier silently handed me a pick and shovel. I racked my brains in an effort to understand what was going on, but with little success. I got the idea, however, that someone else was involved. He seemed to be the Schwein they were talking about, and he seemed to have gone missing.

Finally the officer mounted the jeep beside the driver, and we moved off, everyone on the site watching curiously. The jeep turned left at the crossroads, away from the route I had taken earlier. After a few minutes I saw some German soldiers standing in the road ahead, and when we reached them, the jeep stopped. From the discussion which followed, I gathered that the Schwein was still missing, and it occurred to me that perhaps this was the Germans' name for a British soldier who had been caught, and who perhaps I was to bury. Or, of course, there was the other possibility, I thought dolefully; I was to dig a grave for myself, or even for both of us.

The discussion about the Schwein went on and on, and my forebodings and alarm increased steadily. At last, it seemed to be agreed that the missing Schwein must have gone further along the road, and so the jeep set off once more, this time at a very slow pace while the German soldiers walked with us and closely scanned the passing fields. At last exclamations of excitement showed they had found what they were looking for, and we stopped once more. I was ordered to get down out of the jeep—and then immediately up again to collect the pickaxe and shovel; and now I knew for certain that I was to be the gravedigger.

The driver and the other soldiers walked away from the road, presumably to examine the Schwein at closer quarters, leaving the officer and one soldier with me. My curiosity overcame my fear and I asked, "Was ist zu begraben?" (What is to be buried?) I spoke in German, as this I had already learnt seemed to produce the best results. But the officer, who was obviously surprised, turned to me sharply and gave me a questioning look. I smiled hopefully at him, and then he said, "Ein Schwein. Das stinkt so!" (A pig. It stinks so!) and he put his fingers expressively to his nose. Then he went on: "Sie sprechen gut Deutsch, Ja. Wo haben Sie gelernt?" (You speak German well. Where did you learn?)

I had started to learn German at school, where, with French it became my favourite subject, and continued my studies at college. I had spoken German frequently before the war both socially and in business, and had belonged to various German clubs in London. I had been a member of a discussion group at the City Literary Institute, where only

German was spoken, and went frequently to services at French and German churches. My first job was as a translator and interpreter with a firm which represented several German instrument manufacturers in the UK, and in the course of my work often had accompanied German engineers on visits to customers. So I had quite a good knowledge of German technical terms as well as of everyday expressions. [1]

All this, however, was irrelevant to my present situation: I had to give an answer to the officer befitting my role as a French farm worker, and I chose one without conscious thought, in a sort of Pavlovian reflex. I had learnt how much nearly all young Germans valued a university education; how they seemed to see it as a social distinction which created a kind of camaraderie among all those who belonged. So I replied, "In der Universität (At university). It struck exactly the right note; the young officer, who had university written all over him, smiled kindly at me.

Just as it looked as if my relationship with him was nicely set up, our conversation was interrupted by the return of the driver, who announced that the Schwein was in the middle of the field by which we were standing. So, carrying pick and shovel, I now followed him to the corpse I was to bury. When we reached it, the elusive porker looked enormous; it lay bloated and distended on its back with its trotters sticking up ludicrously from its balloon-like body. And it smelt as the young officer had described, even worse. He suddenly and in some haste left us, saying as he

---

[1] I recall a pre-war incident that taught me something useful in this respect. One day I was taking a German engineer to King's Cross station; as we walked along the subway from the Metropolitan line, he suddenly barked at me: "FRRHRN". I had never heard the expression before, and gazed at him blankly. He repeated himself several times, each time more urgently, and finally I got the message. "Für Herren" he shouted—"WC!" And because we had to go all the way back down the stairs to the lavatory on the underground platform, the phrase was engraved on my mind for ever.

went that he had arranged a meal for me after the job was done.

Looking at the pig, however, I began to have serious doubts about my ability to do the job at all because of its bulk and awkward position. Nevertheless I was more than happy to know that the grave to be made was for a pig and not for me; and revolting as the job was, I fell to with a will. Sadly I soon discovered that my skill as a gravedigger left much to be desired, and I was forced to expend much energy to disguise my inexperience.

My first guard was a pleasant fellow; he told me that the Kommandatur (Commanding Officer) had objected to the smell of the dead pig, and had given orders that a civilian be found to bury it. I was the first civilian to pass by, he said; but in my heart I knew that the smiling redfaced officer was really responsible for my impressment and that this was his way of teaching Frenchman to smile when he smiled at them.

The guard was changed regularly about every ten minutes, and one who arrived when I had managed to dig a fair-sized pit pointed out kindly that I need not actually touch the carcase with my hands, but could drag it to the pit with the aid of a wire hawser conveniently nearby. I was in no mood to waste time fiddling about with wire hawsers, and instead I drove my pick into the pig's bloated stomach intending to show him how much easier it would be to drag the carcase along that way. The guard stepped quickly back; perhaps startled by my callous violence, but he was certainly very anxious to escape the rush of noisome gas released as the blown-up skin collapsed. I grinned to myself, and repeated the blow on one of the dead animal's hams, by which time the guard, with evident distaste had put himself some distance away.

With a final manipulation of the pick I got the pig's legs well tucked into the pit, and then hastily covered the body with earth. The whole job must have taken about two hours, and truthfully I was not too satisfied with the appearance of the end result. There was a hump on the site about two feet high, and only about six inches of earth covered the body. Several of the sentries had made unflattering comments about the quality of my work, and one shrewd chap said he didn't think I could be a farmer, judging by the way I handled a shovel. This did not worry me much, since if he said anything to the young officer I thought it would merely confirm his impression that I was a cut above the ordinary farming type. However, I thought an excuse would do no harm, so I said that I was accustomed to short-handled shovels, not the long-handled I had just been using. Then I realised with horror that the type of spade I had claimed to be familiar with is normally found only in Great Britain. But the guard merely said: "Gut! Nun essen. Ja?" (Good! Now eat. Yes?), to which I gave a vigorous nod of agreement.

We drove back to the village in the jeep and went up a side street to the detachment's canteen, where I was given a bowl of hot stewed meat and some black bread. The sentry who accompanied me looked after me with great care, and spoke with pride of the quality of the meat; he assured me it was 'Prima Fleisch'. Everyone was very friendly and when I had finished eating I was offered coffee. I could not in fact eat all the meat, and one of the soldiers wrapped up what was left on my plate in some paper for me to take away. There was no suggestion that I was not free to go, so finally I said goodbye and set off on foot along the road back to my bicycle, feeling indeed a little annoyed at not being given a lift back in the jeep.

My good humour was restored, however, when I found the bicycle undisturbed, just as I had left it; it did in fact take me some little time to locate it, I had hidden it so well!

Finally, after a delay of three or four hours, but with a good meal inside me, I resumed my journey towards the coast. That night again I had no difficulty in finding shelter, this time in a small side road just beyond Gisors, a market town about halfway between Beauvais and the river Seine. Most of the houses here too were deserted; the occupants had obviously left in a hurry, very likely urged to do so by enemy agents, to join the panic-stricken stream of refugees that had blocked the roads of Northern France just before the German advance began.

Arriving when it was already getting dark, I did not bother to look for luxury accommodation; I just wanted a bed quickly. The facilities in the house were somewhat sparse; I could find no bedclothes and there was no food, so I had to use some of the rations I had brought with me. But there was at least fresh water from a tap.

After a simple supper which was all I needed after the good midday army meal, I slept well on a comfortable mattress; I did not undress, for I wanted to make an early start. I woke at dawn, breakfasted off cold rice pudding and boiled egg together in one portion, washed down with cold water, and in excellent spirits was soon bowling along the road towards the river Seine in the early morning sunshine.

SEVEN

The Pontoon Bridge

With the aid of my Michelin guide, I made good progress towards the river Seine, and as I approached it began to think seriously about how to tackle a problem which had been worrying me for some time. I reckoned that all the bridges would be blown; in which case, of course, I could swim across. But how to get the bicycle over?

Sure enough, when the Seine came into view, near Vernon, about halfway between Rouen and Paris, a ruined bridge dominated the scene. The road runs parallel to the river at this point, and I examined it for about a quarter of a mile each side of the wrecked bridge to see if there were any other ways of getting across, perhaps a boat or another, undamaged, bridge; but I found neither.

Disconsolately I returned to the bridge to have a closer

look. If there was any hope of repair work being under-taken, it might be worth waiting for a few days. But there was no sign of activity of any sort there. I went down to the river bank, and then saw something which was invisible from the road: about a hundred yards upstream, a German military engineer detachment was building a pontoon bridge. I watched fascinated; work was proceeding at great speed, German soldiers swarming all over the structure. All the pontoons seemed to be in position and connected to each other by timber beams, but the laying of planks to form the roadway was still in progress. Clearly, not even military traffic was yet being allowed to cross, so the chances for a civilian must be non-existent.

I needed time to think, and remounting my bicycle, rode away along the riverside road. Would it be worth waiting until the new bridge was finished, I wondered. At the rate the Germans were working it should only be a matter of a day or two before it was open. But if I did wait, would I be given permission to use it? If not, there would have been no point in hanging about. Then it occurred to me that I might ask the officer in charge whether, when the bridge was opened, civilians would be allowed on it. I could decide what to do in the light of his answer.

I returned without delay to the pontoon bridge to seek out the officer in charge. On arrival, I very cautiously approached the incline from the bank to the first pontoon and looked for someone to ask. Nobody took the slightest notice of me, so I trundled my bicycle up the ramp on to the deck of the first pontoon, confident that there I would find an officer.

One or two of the soldiers looked up as I passed, but did not pause in their work or say anything to me. Soon I was on the deck of the first pontoon; still no one asked what I was doing, so I went steadily on, and in a minute reached the far side of the pontoon and crossed to the next. Here even more soldiers seemed to be at work; they lined both

sides of the decking, and all of them were totally uninter-
ested in me. I went on, and to my amazement at each
pontoon had the same experience: the few men to look up
appeared not to see me and returned at once to their work.

I crossed the whole length of the new bridge, and reached
the ramp leading down to the opposite bank without once
being questioned or setting eyes on a single officer. At last,
however, I saw one approaching and, stopping at once,
waited politely for him to reach me. He said nothing about
my not being allowed on the bridge, but in a friendly way
asked what part of the country I came from. Believing that
the further away I said I'd started the better, and also to
justify the direction in which I was heading, I replied, in
French of course, that I was going home to Brittany after
working in the north. The German spoke French fluently,
but as soon as I mentioned Brittany his face lit and he
replied in perfect English: "As you come from Brittany I
suppose you speak English." I would have liked time to
think out the right answer to that, but had to do the best I
could on the spur of the moment, and said without any
hesitation, and in what I hoped was a halting accent: "Yees.
Aiee spik aee leetle Angleesh."

This proved a good answer, the officer grinning at me as
if we shared a secret joke. I grinned back, and he stepped
back, gesturing that I might proceed. I mounted my bicycle,
and with waves and smiles I was on my way—having
crossed the river Seine, almost certainly the first person to
benefit from the Germans' new bridge. It was a demonstration, I thought, of how useful a little bare-faced cheek
could be.

I went on into Vernon, and near the centre of the town
came on a fine house set back in a courtyard, entered
through an imposing iron gate which stood open. I went in
and made a quick check, finding to my delight that the place
was quite empty. In the middle of the courtyard, separated
from the house, was a cellar lodge, probably originally

designed for the porter, with the entrance at the foot of a short flight of steps leading down. The door was open, and when I went in, I found that the walls of the cellar were lined with shelves, stacked with row upon row of bottles. It took me only a few moments to discover that all the bottles contained cider of various types, still and sparkling, and that all of them looked, and proved to be, eminently drinkable. Uplifted at the idea of working my way round at least a part of the stock, I was soon seated comfortably at a table sampling the vintages. There were wide windows, and from where I sat I had a good view of the courtyard and the street outside. I could see German troops passing the entrance, some on foot, some in trucks. Several paused as they went by, and looked enquiringly through the gate but none came in and I was left quite undisturbed for the rest of the afternoon and evening. I made myself very much at home, enjoying a mostly liquid meal, and stayed in the lodge for the night, sleeping like a log. In the morning I was tempted to remain for another day, and even toyed with the idea of setting up a trestle table at the entrance and dispensing cider to passers-by; but finally I decided not to press my luck too far, and set off again in high spirits, taking a few bottles with me as mementoes.

There were few signs of civilian life in Vernon, but as I rode on southwest the countryside began to take on a more normal appearance, the farms being worked and the civilian population carrying on with business as usual. Consequently I had difficulty that evening in finding a deserted house in which to spend the night. I passed through Evreux and Verneuil without finding a place, and finally as it began to get dark reached Alençon. Here all the houses along the main street were clearly occupied; the town seemed unaffected by the war, even the gendarmes being in evidence as though everything was normal. This worried me, for I knew that if I encountered one, he would realise I was English as soon as I opened my mouth.

I carried on through the town, and was in open country once more, when down a lane which appeared to lead to a farmhouse I saw a barn with its doors standing open. Although it was now nearly dark, I could see a loaded haycart inside; and this, I thought, offered the best shelter I was likely to find.

The barn was empty, a ladder leaning against the cart. I climbed it swiftly, and soon made myself comfortable in the soft hay. Before I had settled down, however, I heard a rustling below, followed by the sound of someone climbing the ladder. Then the head of a girl appeared; she did not seem surprised to see me, but asked quite calmly what I was doing. I needed somewhere to sleep, I replied; would it be all right if I stayed the night? I went on to say I hoped I would not cause any one inconvenience. I felt pleased with the French expression I used, which seemed to me just right for the occasion: "J'espére ça ne vous derangerait pas!," I said, although whether it was correct French or not I did not know. Correct or otherwise, it had the desired effect: the girl smiled, and said it would be quite all right if I stayed. Then she left, taking her time, it seemed to me. But perhaps that was just wishful thinking. I believe she had guessed I was English.

Next day was a Sunday, and I continued my journey without incident, my navigation faultlessly directed by the invaluable Michelin. I passed Mayenne, and in the afternoon reached the city of Rennes, where there was virtually no sign at all that a war was on. The entire population seemed to be out, promenading in its Sunday best, and I felt very much the unwanted stranger, as I walked through the town centre, the dust of the journey mixed with the sweat on my face, and my clothes shabby and unkempt. I kept to the edge of the pavement, wheeling my bicycle along the gutter—the main street through the town being steeply uphill made it hard work—and not surprisingly the towns-folk, who all appeared to me, to be most elegantly dressed, gave me a wide berth. It was not surprising that I earned scornful looks; I felt like a pariah—and probably looked like one too.

It was a relief to leave the place and the atmosphere of make-believe which enveloped it. Out in the countryside once more, though still deep in hostile territory, I felt in myself a sense of real freedom, which cheered me greatly.

My elation was mainly due to the fact that at last I was approaching my main objective, the sea. The Brittany coast lies northwest from Rennes, and I took Route Nationale N12 out of the city, Michelin indicating that this way I could avoid St Malo, which I thought was too big a port for an escape attempt. My hope was to find a fishing harbour where security was not too strict, and in which I might chance on a small unguarded fishing boat. I rode via Yffiniac to St Brieuc, about 35 miles west of St Malo, and itself also too big for my purpose; but in the town there is a turning off the N12 which heads northwest towards a number of small coastal villages, and I reckoned that in one of these I might find what I was looking for.

The anticipation of reaching the sea spurred me on my way, but before I did so I had again to find somewhere to sleep. When dusk approached I was about halfway from Rennes to St Brieuc, and as once more there appeared to be no empty houses anywhere, I decided to bed down in a haystack for the second time. I found one without much difficulty just off the road by a field gate, and tired after a long day, settled down in it and was quickly and soundly asleep. Next morning, in good spirits, despite having only a cold breakfast of food from my haversack, I continued on my journey to St Brieuc and the sea. It was the 16th June, six days since I had left Boursies.

EIGHT

Brittany and a Boat

At St Brieuc I had my first glimpse of the sea, but I did not dally, and took the road suggested by Michelin, which was signposted to Paimpol. After riding for about thirty solitary minutes I came to a fishing village called Binic, and feeling tired, for I had come a long way from the haystack, lay down for a rest in the sunshine in a grass field with my bicycle in the nearby ditch. I promptly fell fast asleep, but quite soon something or someone woke me, and opening my eyes, I saw a circle of a dozen or so wide-eyed men, women and children standing round me and gazing at me in complete silence. I felt like Gulliver waking up in Lilliput. There was a man who looked like a farmer, the others I guessed were his family, with some farmworkers as well.

I had fallen asleep, innocently enough, lying on my back

with my arms folded under my head as a pillow, and as I struggled back to consciousness, I realised that my well-displayed army boots were attracting a lot of attention. I feared that they might identify me as a soldier on the run, but when the man I assumed to be the head of the family spoke, it was to ask me if I would like to come to his house for some cider—an invitation too welcome for me to be doubtful about.

We all walked together to his house—the farm—and had hardly sat down when the local priest arrived, out of breath as though he had been running. I guessed that he had been summoned to give me a look-over, so I told him the story that I had previously adopted: that I came from the north, near the Belgian border, adding, to account for my accent, that my mother was Flemish. He did not say whether he believed me, but I had a feeling he did not and that he probably suspected I was English. His manner was cool initially, and became more so as we talked, as did that of the family. I began to fear that they might think I was a Gestapo agent, but found subsequently that a cold welcome for strangers was normal in the area, and I adopted a correspondingly close manner.

In the end, I left this isolated farmhouse without hindrance or help, and again had to find a place to sleep. I found some ruins of a monastery I think, well hidden in a wood behind the small harbour, where I spent a rather damp night. In the next few days I thoroughly but cautiously explored the coast westwards, visiting most of the harbours as far as Paimpol, where from the quayside I was able to observe a small German naval air-sea rescue launch at close quarters. How marvellous it would be to board her and make off across Channel, I thought. But such an idea was strictly of the Walter Mitty school and I did not seriously consider it.

Exploration was a slow business, made slower because I could not risk being seen too often in the same place; but finally I decided that the small fishing harbour of Brehet between Plouha and Plouezec looked suitable for my purpose, and during the next eight days I made myself familiar with the layout both of the Brehet harbour and its landward approaches. During this time, I constantly changed my sleeping place. I was glad to leave the ruins which were very uncomfortable when it rained, the only shelter being a large stone slab (it turned out to be a tomb-stone), for much better accommodation in the garden shed of an empty house. Unfortunately, however, a woman came every day to tend the garden, and the place was inconveniently located. So another move followed and then another and I found myself changing so often that I no longer remember where they all were.

I did not succeed in breaking the ice with any of the local fishermen, despite hours spent hanging around the harbour and nearby fishing beaches. In fact, I hardly ever saw anyone and began to think people were deliberately keeping out of my way. There were other strangers in the area, refugees from the war zones, but they lived communally and kept themselves to themselves. Sometimes I saw them busy cooking a meal with single-minded concentration, as I passed by, but they took no interest in me, which was not surprising. Their difficulties, living in make-shift quarters and unwanted by the local people, were real enough to occupy all their attention. After a while I adopted the pretence that I was such a refugee myself: it was a good cover against any interest on the part of the gendarmes.

I had to do some shopping from time to time, and in order to arouse as little curiosity as possible, distributed my custom over a wide area, my bicycle making this easy. I bought a map of the district, a torch and a small compass, for use once I found a boat and was sea-borne. It was to prove a poor investment, however, being only a simple pivoted needle type which, with the movement of the waves, would swing round continually, showing all the points of the compass in turn. However it taught me the need for a liquid compass, which was a valuable lesson for future planning.

Hanging round the harbour and shopping, of course, occupied only a small part of my time. Mostly I was exploring Brehet and its hinterland. The harbour was set in a small inlet between high cliffs to the west, and, on the east, a low bank on which a few cottages stood back from the water. The inlet was about a hundred yards long and at its head was a short quay behind which were a few more cottages.

The cliffs on the west side could only be climbed with some difficulty for there was no proper path from the beach, though there was a little used one from a road about a quarter of a mile inland leading up to the summit. The cliffs gave on to unused moorland, and I decided that the cliff top would be an ideal place where to assemble a store of the necessities for the voyage to England, which increasingly seemed a viable proposition. It would be conveniently near to the water despite the long climb, so that loading a boat when I found one would not be too difficult. I started my cache without delay; from it I had a good view of the harbour and could thus examine at my leisure the five or six boats moored there. In due course I would have to decide which one to try to escape in.

The moorings, I noticed, were made to the sandy bottom of the inlet, for there was no harbour wall to which they could be tied up anywhere near. There was a wall at the extreme landward end of the inlet, but the bottom there was dry at low tide, and only two or three boats, which I never saw being used, were moored there. The boats further out that I had my eye on were just afloat at low tide, which was when I should want to sail, aiming to get away on a good easterly current, as the water flooded up the Channel.

I always approached Brehet harbour and the neighbouring beaches from the landward side, for I thought that it might arouse suspicion if I were often seen moving along

the exposed coast. This made my movements both complicated and time-consuming, since Brehet lies at the con-
fluence of five or six valleys which run down to the sea from
the nearby hills. So, for example, when I wanted to go from
my cache on the cliffs west of the harbour to the high ground
behind the cottages on the eastern side of the harbour, a
distance of about 200 yards, I had to make a journey of four
miles. And before I could do this I had to learn the winding
routes of the footpaths across each of the five or six valleys. I
often comforted myself during the wearisome business by
recalling the old army maxim: time spent on reconnaissance
is seldom wasted.

The problem of finding a source of drinking water for the
voyage to put into the cache was a major headache, for
there was no public supply. After many hours of searching I
located a spring in a small hamlet in the hills behind Brehet,
from which a continuous flow of clear water poured into a
basin set in a wall below; and for storing it I found some
empty litre bottles in a shed. But the shed was about five
miles from my cache. I calculated that eight litres of water
would be the minimum requirement for a journey which
might last seven days, and collecting, filling and conveying
so many bottles to my store was a seemingly endless task,
for I carried only two bottles at a time so as not to attract
attention.

I still had a few tins of meat from Boursies, and I used
these and some of the tins I had acquired from various
empty houses on my journey, as the foundation of my
store. I supplemented them with vegetables—cabbage,
turnips and so on—which I gathered from fields in the
neighbourhood, and also with crêpes, one of the specialities
of the region, of which I bought sufficient to last me at sea, I
hoped, for a week.

Meanwhile, I ate at a small wayside café, most days
having 'soupe', made mainly of cabbage water and meat
stock, crêpes, and occasionally an omelette, washed down

with cider. As a treat I sometimes finished with coffee and a cognac. This cost the incredibly modest sum, even for 1940, of two sous, or less than a farthing (1/8p)!

Clothing for the voyage was another major problem, for I knew I might face all kinds of weather conditions. In the house adjoining the shed in which for a time I slept, I found a sheet of canvas, and some tar. By painting the canvas with tar I made a tarpaulin, which I hoped would give me some protection from waves breaking over the vessel and from rain. I also found two blankets, some items of clothing, and a few groceries there. I had to steal most things I needed and my skill in this art improved rapidly. I developed a pride in the neatness of my work, learning quickly to vacate a house without leaving evidence of a break-in to be reported to the gendarmes with whom I dare not risk a confrontation.

At last, my preparations were sufficiently advanced to allow me to move to a spot near my cache in the gorse overlooking the harbour. I decided that the most suitable boat there for my purpose was a small fishing smack, about 10 feet long, with one mainsail and a foresail, but no engine, which was moored nearest to the edge of the water under the cliff. I went down to the beach to examine it with great care at different stages of the tide, and found that at low tide it remained just afloat and would be easy to board and untie. I learnt by heart the precise positions of the sails, sheets and mooring lines, as well as the exact locations of the rudder eyebolts and rings, so that I could board the vessel and prepare for sea in the dark. I quite believed that I was ready to set sail for home whenever the wind was favourable, and gave no thought to the effects of the Channel currents on an unpowered boat, nor to any restrictions there might be on the movement of craft in this area, or, for that matter, to the reaction of the owner, who in all this time had made no visit to his vessel.

Although the wind had been fair and regular from the south all the time I was at Brehet, it dropped almost completely on the night I chose for my get-away and I was compelled to abandon my plans for at least 24 hours, which was very hard to bear, for after weeks of anticipation I was now keyed up with excitement. But I had no alternative. To make matters worse, I had spent all my money and so the next day, while I waited, it meant eating some of the stock of food I had prepared for the journey. Next night there was still little wind, but in my eagerness to be off I decided to take a chance, hoping the wind would freshen out at sea.

First I had to dispose of my trustworthy bicycle that had served me so well, without fault of any description, not even a puncture, on that unlikely ride through the quiet French countryside all the way from Boursies. I took it to the cliff top where I regretfully laid it down, a few yards from the edge, feeling I was losing an old friend. Its resting place was amongst flowering heather, and that comforted me a little.

With that simple act I seemed also to cast-off the unhappy role of a nameless, homeless, and near penniless refugee, and to assume once more that of a soldier still on active service. I had no weapons, and no papers, little more than those boots to which I had become indissolubly attached, but I did have a strong resurgence of my determination to get back into the action, and that, as I had resolved all along, by way of the sea. It was only the sea, now, which separated me from England. Down there, in the quiet, deserted harbour, was a vessel capable of taking me there. All that was now required was some concentrated silent activity, and the continued absence of any interest on the part of the local fishermen, and the gendarmes, and above all, of the German patrols.

With extra caution now, I walked to my cache to collect my stores, carried them down to the harbour, ready to stow in the boat I had chosen. Everything was going according to plan; the tide was just right at low, the boat just afloat, and it was easy to reach it by wading across the sandy bottom. My softly squelchy steps made no more sound than my thumping heart.

NINE

Round the Channel Islands

I succeeded in boarding the boat and stowed my quite extensive stores without mishap and in relative silence, despite its lying some twelve to fifteen yards out from the shore and my having to take my boots and socks off to wade to it. My next job was to fit the rudder into its eyebolts, a task that I had worried about more than any other, for it was difficult enough to manage it in daylight, and I feared it might be almost impossible in darkness. The rudder had to be lowered over the stern, and the pins and eyebolts by which it was fixed to the hull, engaged by feel; but I had studied their positions with great care whenever the tide was low enough, and had them clearly fixed in my mind so that I could picture their positions. Gratifyingly the rudder slipped neatly into place at my first attempt, and after that, casting off was easy. I did not think I should need the mooring line, so after loosening it I just let it drop into the water.

The only worrying sound came from the pulley blocks squeaking as I hoisted sail, but there was no sign that anyone heard and in a few minutes the boat was moving freely away from the shore, leaving behind a phosphorescent trail of bubbles, which seemed so bright that I was afraid they might be seen from the quayside. Although I worried about them, they were at the same time a source of great satisfaction, for they were visible proof that at last I was really on my way. My every thought and action had been focused on this moment for so long that now it had come to pass the effect on me was almost mystical. In the elation of the moment I quite forgot that my feet and trouser legs were soaking wet; but soon they began to chill and I had to give them some attention.

As the boat moved out of the little cove the wind freshened slightly from the southwest, which I thought encouraging, for at least it was blowing in the right direction. It was about midnight when I sailed, and at first light I saw that I was well away from land and the boat making good progress eastwards. The morning passed quickly for I was very busy, keeping a constant watch for landmarks, the position of which I had memorised from the map, checking the sun's position, and frequently examining the boat's gear and rigging. The wind dropped after a while, then the calm was broken by occasional gusts which blew from all quarters, and finally it returned to the southwest. I thought I was making good progress, until shortly after midday, when I realised with a shock that I was no longer sailing east but was being carried back on my tracks—and soon at an alarming rate.

Presently I recognised a promontory west of the bay from which I had started, and I was well past it before the boat's direction reversed once again, and began to move eastwards. By then it was late afternoon, and the bitter truth of the situation finally dawned on me: my boat, however skilled the helmsman, could not be sailed effectively against the forces of sea and wind in which it was trapped, and was being helplessly carried backwards and forwards, like flotsam, by the tide.

There is a kind of bottleneck in the English Channel at this point, where the tide sweeps in and out through virtual narrows between the Cherbourg peninsula and the Isle of Wight, washing over the rocky outcrops of the Channel Islands as it does so. The biggest of these outcrops is the Minquiers plateau, between Jersey and St Malo; I just saw one of the markers indicating the plateau before the boat was turned by the tide and began to travel back to the west. It was so large and had such an elaborate superstructure that I was not sure whether in fact it was a buoy or a beacon. It was, in fact, a buoy, and there are—or were in 1940—six of them sited round the outer perimter of the plateau, which covers an area of some thirty square miles. I thought, however, that there were only three, anchored in a line running roughly north to south, of which the one I saw was the most southerly.

As the afternoon wore on I was carried back to the Minquiers, this time with the aid of the wind which had considerably strengthened and enabled me to go against the tide, and by evening I could again see the southernmost buoy, rapidly increasing in size as I approached it in the failing light. It was then that I thought of a way in which I might beat the elements, by tying up to it while the tide was running out west, and casting off again when it ran back; but it was not until I drew near to the buoy that I began even faintly to appreciate the full force of the tidal flow. Water seethed round its base like a mill-race, creating a heaving depression some ten feet deep on the downstream side; and to tie up to it looked well-nigh impossible. Twice I tried and failed, the strength of the current each time tearing the line from my hands; but at the third attempt I managed to get a

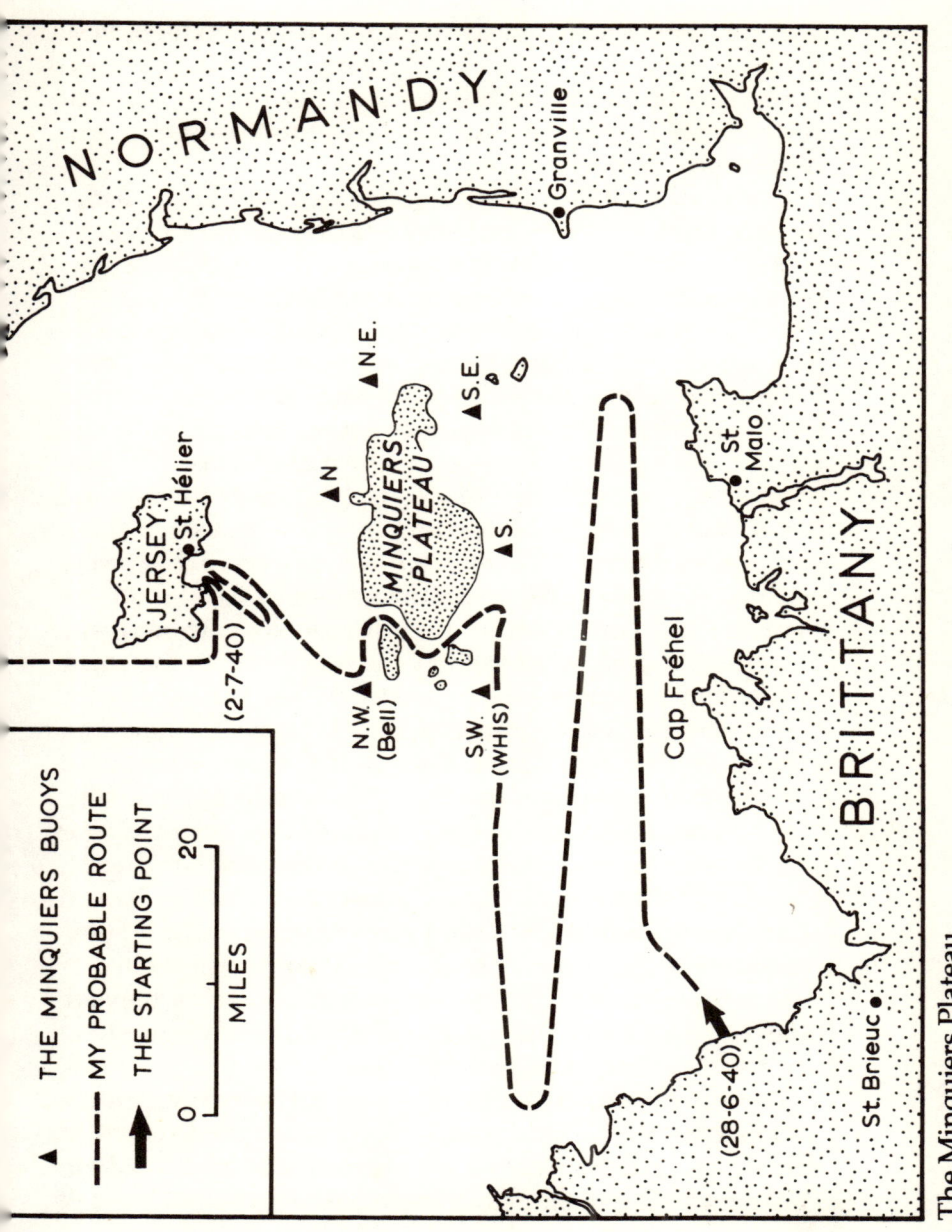

NORMANDY

Granville

N.E.

S.E.

JERSEY
St. Hélier

N

MINQUIERS PLATEAU

S.

St. Malo

BRITTANY

(2-7-40)

N.W. (Bell)

S.W. (WHIS)

Cap Fréhel

▲ THE MINQUIERS BUOYS

– – – MY PROBABLE ROUTE

↑ THE STARTING POINT

0   20
MILES

(28-6-40)

St. Brieuc

The Minquiers Plateau

hitch on while the boat was still under way, and then, very quickly, lowered the sail. That accomplished, it was relatively easy to put three heavy ropes out to hold the boat secure, leaving enough slack to allow it to toss freely, clear of the buoy's side.

The sketch map of the Minquiers Plateau which, also, I did not have at this crucial stage, shows the position of all six buoys. It can be seen that there are only two buoys in a north-south line, these being marked SW (WHIS) and NW (BELL); a third, marked N, is a good deal further east. The presumed course of my journey is also marked. At the time I knew little about the vast area of reefs and rocks, and the terrifying night I was to spend being washed around it did not add much to my knowledge. The movements of its tidal streams are in fact extremely complex. They rip over and across the plateau at high tide, but at low water take on a circular motion round it. Each of the six buoys were positioned some three to six miles from the edge of the plateau, and consequently the flow of the current at the buoys is not directly affected by the tide rips over the edges of the plateau, but is determined by the general state of the tide in the English Channel; there are however secondary effects in the area, caused by water being channelled through rock formations in the plateau, known as overfalls. The first buoy I tied up to, the Southwest Minquiers, is near the Brisants du Sud rocks, and the second, the Northwest, guards the Brisants du Nord Ouest, rocks which remain submerged even at low tide. I have never discovered how the buoys were moored to the rocky bottom in twelve or fifteen fathoms of water, and cannot imagine how they are able to withstand the tidal forces constantly smashing against their considerable bulk.

The buoy's superstructure was about twelve feet high, and incorporated a ladder to the top. I managed to crawl on to the base, and then found it quite easy to climb the ladder; I was rewarded with a faint view of the grey silhouette of

Jersey in the far distance, with what appeared to be several large warships lying offshore. About midway between the warships and my own position, I thought I could make out another buoy, and I decided to make this my next target, and endeavour, on reaching it, to tie up once more.

Feeling well pleased with my reconnaissance, I returned to the boat, and wrapped myself up in the blankets amidships to pass as comfortable a night as possible in the haphazard pitching and tossing to which, now that it was stationary, it was subjected. The siren of the buoy (designated in the marine chart as a whistle) was operated by the action of the waves, on some kind of bellows, and it gave forth an eerie irregular boom, varying from very gentle wheezes to deafening roars. In the fitful half-sleep into which I fell it seemed to be talking to me in a sorrowful tone: "You're young, v-e-r-y y-o-u-n-g, v-e-r-y y-o-u-n-g," it said. "G-o-i-n-g to d-i-e. G-o-i-n-g to d-i-e. O-o-o-mph! (as if it had indigestion) "G-i-r-l-s, G-i-r-l-s—I like g-i-r-l-s. O-o-o-mph!"

When I woke it was still dark, and I felt a pleasant sensation of gently drifting, with no more of the rough pitching and tossing. I revelled in it for a few moments, not wanting to end it by finding out the true state of affairs; then I realised that I could no longer hear the siren, and when I looked out the buoy was nowhere in sight. Now I understood why it was so calm. My mooring ropes had parted and I was adrift in the dark.

Although at first I could see nothing, I could clearly hear the sound of water lapping, splashing, sluicing and breaking, and realised unhappily that I was being washed around the rocks and ridges of the Minquiers plateau itself. Gradually, as my eyes became accustomed to the dark, I made out the shape of a long black ridge in the gloom. At first I thought it might be a bank of seaweed, but it was too high and regular in outline for that; perhaps it was an outcrop of rock or an exposed reef.

The noise of rushing water and swirling waves seemed to increase, and as time went on I began to perceive a pattern of heaving swells on the surface of the sea, barely visible yet indefinably sinister. I felt that I was in a dreadful dream world, being swept around in the swirling water—and then I distinguished streaks and patches of white in the darkness, and realised that I was looking at surf and spume cascading off unseen rocks.

When it was light enough to see I discovered that one of the buoys was still in the offing although in the morning mist I could not tell which. Later, as the mist began to clear, I found that I had drifted a considerable distance east during the night, and was now some way beyond St Malo; I could recognise some of the coastal features, in particular a white cliff which I took to be Cap Frehel. This proved a useful eastern landmark for the rest of the day. With much backtracking, and frequent lulls as Gulf Stream cyclones passed over, I progressed slowly northwards during the daylight hours, at the same time continuing to be pushed alternately east and west as the tide changed.

By evening, despite all the backtracking, I had reached the next buoy north from my previous night's anchorage, which I could see clearly, a mile or two away, possibly more. I tied up to it as before, finding the current still flowing fast southwest so that the boat's bows faced northeast. This time I used the anchor chain and several additional ropes to make fast, in an effort to prevent another breakaway. I had progressed one beacon's distance since morning, which was some progress at least. But it was not enough: in two days I had achieved only one-eighth of my journey.

Some time during the night, a star check told me that the moored boat had swung round and was facing south, which meant that the current had changed and was now running up Channel, towards the northeast. I cast off without a moment's delay, quite confident that after the experience I'd already gained I could handle the boat in the dark; all being well, my course would now in any case be well away from the treacherous Minquiers.

With both the tide and wind for once in my favour, I realised that I must fast be approaching Jersey; and sure enough, in the half light of early morning, I saw ahead of me emerging through the mist a sublime vision of rose-coloured cliffs seemingly suspended in mid air. I felt that I was looking at a painter's dream of a magic sunrise; and the painting grew steadily in scale and grandeur as I drew nearer to the island. Soon, on the starboard bow, the upper half of a lighthouse appeared, illuminated by the rays of the still obscured sun, which I guessed must be the lighthouse at La Corbiere, west of St Helier. Against the fantastic backdrop of coloured cliffs and gleaming archways it glowed, a rose-red tower floating in the mists of eternity. I sat motionless in my boat, gazing in awe at the mystical beauty of the scene—and in some indefinable way, stirred by coming so close to the mysterious and fathomless power of the elements.

Soon however, there were more immediate concerns to occupy my mind. I was horrified to discover, as the air began slowly to clear, that the vision which so moved me was slowly receding from view; finally it merged once more into the mists, and when much later, the air completely cleared, only the distant grey silhouette of Jersey remained on the horizon. I was being taken away off course again, westward, and all I could do was to try to coax my inadequate little craft on as northerly a course as possible, against a tide now running once more strongly southwards.

It was a miserable task. Frequent cyclones passed over during the day, each one taking about an hour and depriving me of all assistance from the wind while it lasted. The poor sailing qualities of the boat were no help. It was not possible to tack her, owing, I discovered, to a layer of concrete about a foot thick which lined the bilges in the bottom of her hull, so that virtually all I could do was to let her sail with the wind, and attempt, with a touch on the rudder occasionally, to urge her in the right direction. It was like trying to sail a log of wood. Soon it was clear that once again the boat was being carried helplessly at the mercy of the tide. Not till the afternoon did the flood tide flow again, and then I came spanking back to Jersey, aided by the wind which was now blowing full from the south.

As I came into St Helier bay, I was overjoyed at the sight of a small dinghy some distance from the shore with three fishermen aboard pulling up crab pots. As I approached them, I waved, grinning complacently, and shouted in English, "I suppose there aren't any Jerries here yet!" The answer was a most unwelcome shock. "Yes. They came yesterday!" And the fishermen indicated vigorously that I should keep away from the port, pointing excitedly out to the west as my route. I did not stop to ask questions but immediately swung the boat round in its tracks and headed in the direction they had shown, badly shaken by the news but thankful that I had been warned in time, and had not sailed in ignorance straight into the enemy's hands.[1]

I was in two minds about taking the fishermen's advice and steering west, for England lay due north; but at first there was no alternative, for I was off the southern coast of Jersey and had to get round the island. So I had perforce to head west, observing as I went a few German aircraft, engaged it seemed in a rather desultory patrol of the coast-line, but too high to make any detailed examination, and certainly not of such a small craft as mine.

Once round the southwestern extremity, I decided to disregard the fishermen's advice and head north once more. The wind held south, and soon I was making good

[1] The Germans arrived in Jersey on the 1st July, so I must have been there on the 2nd July in St Helier Bay. The warships I had seen from the top of the buoy two evenings earlier were probably British vessels evacuating troops and island personnel.

headway; by nightfall I had passed Sark. The night was uneventful, and although I had no means of checking my position, I felt reasonably satisfied that I was on course, and making good some of the lost time. At dawn, to starboard I could just see the west coast of Normandy; and there was a small blur ahead which I took to be Alderney.

My spirits rose: in the last 24 hours I had covered a greater distance than in the whole of the first three days. When I was planning my journey in Brehet I envisaged it in three stages, the first to Alderney, the most northerly of the Channel Islands, the second thence halfway across the Channel, and the third the remaining distance to England. After I had satisfied myself that the island ahead was indeed Alderney, I reckoned that before the end of the day I should be well into the second stage of my voyage, this being the fourth day since leaving Brittany. Further, for the first time since sailing, I did not feel sea-sick. I had some meat and a crêpe, which I greatly enjoyed, even though the crêpe was sodden with sea water. With a good meal inside me, and the renewed hope of a successful conclusion to my voyage, my optimism reached its highest point of the day. By nightfall I was past Alderney and to my reckoning almost certainly a good ten miles out into the Channel. Not having eaten anything for three days I must have been in a low state of health and not willing to contemplate anything other than an early and successful conclusion to the whole affair. Passing through the straits between Alderney and France had been accomplished with complete success: no sign of any enemy ships, no challenge from the shore, and wind and tide in my favour. I did not know that I was sailing in some of the most dangerous waters in the world, and that this might have been the reason for my not having encountered any German patrols.

As night fell, the wind held south and with good visibility I was able to continue steering due north with the aid of the stars for my bearings in the dark; if my navigation was accurate, the course should bring me up near the Isle of Wight. I passed the time seated in the stern of the boat, half dozing, with the tiller under my arm. The cramped position became increasingly uncomfortable as the hours crept by, and I longed to stretch my legs, and ease my aching back; but any relief was out of the question owing to the narrow space. To pass the time, I concentrated my mind on the three stages into which I had divided my journey. I was satisfied that I was now well out into mid-Channel and accordingly I reckoned that I must now be approaching stage three, the last.

I was at first encouraged when heavier seas began to run, tossing the little craft about like the proverbial cork—far too violently for comfort. I thought they would be Atlantic rollers sweeping into mid-Channel. Although after a time the violence of the waves became frightening, I still remained cheerful at the thought of being near home at last. My fond hopes were abruptly dashed, however, when a wave broke clean over the stern of the boat and drenched me from head to foot; and when a second wave overwhelmed the craft I was totally dazed and soon began to shiver, for the wind had become bitterly cold. I altered course westwards to avoid the stern-pooping (waves breaking over the stern) and the water pouring into the craft, and by this means I suffered no further dowsings. But the remainder of the night was a nightmare: ceaselessly I had to struggle to avoid high banks of ominous black rollers sweeping up from astern, and walls of angry white foam coming in from the after-quarters. Some of the waves seemed stationary: the position of one remained unchanged in relation to the boat for the rest of the night.

With the dawn, my spirits suffered a final, knockout blow. Ahead of me in the morning light loomed an island. At first I tried to convince myself that there must be a gap in my education, that an island existed in the middle of the English Channel of which I had never heard. But at last I had to admit to what I had all along known in my heart: that I was approaching Alderney again, and from the south at that. The boat had been washed back south right round the island, quite possibly over the dangerous Casquet reefs off the west coast. Now I was not moving effectively at all, but to-ing and fro-ing offshore in the unforgiving sea, going nowhere. For more than an hour I was tossed around; then resigning myself to what seemed inevitable, I decided I had had enough, and that the only thing to do was to make my way back to the mainland.

I was in fact in no condition to continue the struggle. Weakened by the night's buffeting, I was shivering continuously and violently, and my teeth were chattering uncontrollably. Sunburn and salt water combined had caused painful sores all over my knees and forearms; the skin of my face was like an overdone steak, my lips were cracked, and my cheeks gaunt and hollow. All my limbs were aching after five nights and four days in the cramped conditions of the little boat; I had no idea what I should do when I reached land. It was a case of first things first, of getting out of the boat and out of the sea in which I had suffered so much. What I would do next would just have to wait.

As soon as I turned the boat towards the mainland, it began to make good progress, being carried in on the tide and the resulting current through the strait between Alderney and the mainland. The Cap de la Hague on the northern shore of the Normandy peninsula slowly became visible, and after rounding it I began to strain my eyes in search of a suitable beach on which to land. Presently I saw ahead of me what I first thought to be a long line of breakers; but it turned out to be a raging spume-flecked torrential current which I learned later was called the Blanchart Race. I blundered into it, and was immediately rewarded with a snapped boom-sheet and severed stays. The force of the waves threw the boat so violently up and down that at one moment the boom was at an angle of 45 degrees to the mast, and in the next it crashed down with such force that all the supporting stays were carried away, and the mainsail collapsed in a flapping heap over the deck and on top of the boom lying athwart the hull. I was only just able to summon up enough strength to get it back in position by improvising a new line with which to hoist it up the mast and secure it with a fresh boom sheet. If I had not succeeded, all control of the boat would have been lost. It all took some time but it had to be done somehow or other.

At one moment the boat might seem to be sailing normally over the surface of the sea, in the next it might drop ten or fifteen feet into a hole in the water, landing at the bottom with a mind-bending crash. I could not understand what was happening: I knew I could not be in a whirlpool, for there was no circular motion as if the boat was caught in the eddy leading to the drop. I spent a night of terror being tossed about in the chaos, and in the morning, glad to be alive, still had no idea where I had been or what had happened. When daylight came I was past caring about anything; all the boat's gear was hopelessly entangled, and all my hopes of soon being home, completely shattered.

I was barely managing to control the boat, and it was only luck that brought it at last between a line of rocks into a pleasant bay, the calm water of which made an incredible contrast to the inferno raging in the water outside. Inland, the countryside looked very peaceful; wooded hills rose behind a shingle beach, and I thought I could hide safely in them for awhile. Before reaching them however, there were still problems to solve. A channel up to the beach took some finding, and with my makeshift sail I floundered about in a most unseamanlike manner for a considerable time. An unseen fisherman witnessed my arrival; he told me later that it was 8 o'clock in the morning, and high tide, when I ran my boat ashore on to the top of the shingle beach. He did not mince his words in describing the way I had sailed in: "Comme une vache!" (like a cow), he said. And such was my appearance that he thought I was an old man.

His name was Mangepin, and I came to know him very well. He was to be the main instrument of my ultimate salvation. [1]

---

[1] I did not know at the time of the existence of the Blanchart Race. It seems that in the neighbourhood of the Cap de la Hague the rocky bottom of the sea-bed is broken by deep holes and equally high outcrops, and that these may be the cause of the sudden changes in water level. There is one deep cleft known as the Hague Ditch where the nautical chart indicates the change in level in the sea bed of 16 fathoms, or 96 feet.

I have never been able to determine whether I travelled round the west side of Alderney, or through the straits on the east side—or perhaps I did both. I may have circled the island before ending south of it in the morning. The reefs, part of the Casquets rocks, lie mainly to the west; the Blanchart Race runs through the straits on the east side of the island.

The tidal currents round Alderney over a 12 hour period gives a maximum speed off the west coast of 7 knots and off the east coast of 6 knots. High tide is about one hour earlier than at Dover and, at −1hour Dover, the current flows in both directions through the straits. The maximum speed of the southward current occurs at 12 hours Dover, or three hours after high tide. From my estimated position in the English Channel at dusk, it would thus seem quite likely that my boat was taken round the west side of the island during the night. There are many strange stories of whirlpools and other mysterious phenomena in the Blanchart Race, and of the wrecks—including that of a French submarine sunk in the early days of the war—that lie on the bottom.

While on the subject of the tidal diagrams, the behaviour of the currents over the Minquiers Plateau may be of interest. The question uppermost in my mind was whether, when the tide turned and began to ebb, the water continued to pour over the top of the plateau or whether at some stage after the reef became exposed, this stopped, and if so did it circle round the reef or pass either side of it. I shall never know, after I came adrift from the buoy on the first night, whether I was washed over the top of the reef or round the edges and through the channels which surround it.

TEN

Normandy and Recovery

I found that the Normandy bay in which I had blundered ashore was the Anse St Martin. As soon as the boat grounded I was out, lowering the sail and stowing it quickly as best I could, then gathering my few remaining belongings into the tarpaulin which I made into a sort of hold-all. As it was high tide the boat had beached at the top of the shingle bank, consequently I only had to go over the top of the beach to get into the nearby field. There was however a stone wall separating the two and owing to my weak state I was unable at first to climb over it. A young girl was driving cows in the field, and as soon as she saw me she made off, leaping like one possessed over the field walls that were in her path. I was far too preoccupied with my own problems to worry about what she might do, although I assumed that

100

she was rushing off to impart the news of what she had seen
coming from the beach. It was only after several attempts
that I finally—and painfully—succeeded in slithering over
the wall. After recovering my breath I began to limp up the
sloping field—and to wonder what tale the girl would tell at
home about the tattered looking devil with a black bag who
had come out of the sea!

Although when I first saw it the hillside behind the beach
had seemed well covered with copses and spinneys in
which I might hide and get warm lying out in the sun, it
turned out not to be so. There were walled gardens seemingly everywhere, and I had to take to a road leading inland,
which ascended steeply until suddenly it came to the outskirts of a small village. This I discovered later was called
Digulleville; as I approached it I saw a few people ahead of
me, one of them a German soldier. My appearance, I knew,
was grotesque, for I had not shaved since leaving Brittany,
and my clothes were in rags and tatters. I was wearing
corduroy trousers which I had cut off raggedly at the knee
in order to get rid of the wet legs resulting from wading to
the boat. My knees were blistered from exposure. I had no
socks on, just the army boots, for these had been soaked at
the same time.

I had at all cost to avoid being seen in such a condition, so
I quickly made myself scarce by clambering over a wall into
a pasture which sloped steeply upwards to a small copse,
into which I disappeared, relieved that I had not been
observed. The sun, which had shone brightly earlier, was
now obscured by clouds, and a cold wind had blown up,
which put paid to any ideas of a comfortable thaw out.

Inside the wood I saw, almost at once, a house which
clearly was in German occupation, with a large petrol
dump, which extended into the wood, set up alongside it.
Clearly the wood was no place for me, so I hid my makeshift
tarpaulin bundle in the undergrowth, detoured cautiously
round the occupied house, and emerged from the wood

once more, full of forebodings of misfortune, to find myself in the main street of the village. Fortunately it was completely deserted, and I continued on past a farmhouse with a yard in the front, which I thought for a moment of entering; but then I heard children's voices shouting in play at the back and hurried on. A few steps later a dog barked at me, and I cursed it under my breath. And then a door opened, and a strikingly beautiful woman of middle age looked out, and at once fixed her eyes on me.

I went up to her and asked, with a little preamble, if she could help me with an old pair of reasonably presentable trousers—"de vieux pantalons", I said. Without a word, this admirable lady turned back into her house, and returned almost at once with a pair of blue cotton trousers, which she silently handed to me. Then: would I like a drink of water and a wash, she enquired, and I replied yes, please, without hesitation.

As I followed her, she asked almost at once if I was English. At first I denied it, but she pressed me, and then briefly I told her my story. Soon her husband came in, and I repeated it to him. After I had finished, this wonderful couple offered to keep me with them till I was fully recovered, and able to put to sea again. Their name was Beauchaux, and for a whole week they laboured to get me on my feet again. For the first two days I slept solidly in the luxury of soft mattress and clean linen without waking. Then I began to think of the future and what my next move should be. I was well aware that despite their kindness I could not prolong my stay with my new friends indefinitely, for my presence would in the end almost certainly be discovered by the Germans, with disastrous consequences for my benefactors.

The danger of discovery was all the more real, I soon appreciated, since the room the Beauchaux gave me had been listed by the Germans as an officer's billet; at any time someone might come to inspect it or even to announce the arrival of an occupant. Mme Beauchamp said, however, when I raised the matter with her, that there was no immediate need for me to go: she was sure no one knew I was there, she had looked carefully up and down the street when we first spoke and there had been no one in sight; but if I went out, I must be extremely careful to make sure I was not seen leaving or entering the house. It was part of a terrace, but it had a door to the backgarden, in which was the lavatory, just an enclosure without a roof; an umbrella was placed in a handy position for use when it rained. Behind the garden was a field, and behind the field, a little-used lane, and this was my route when I started to go out.

M. Beauchaux was a retired policeman, although from what branch of the service I never discovered; I think perhaps it might have been the Sûreté in Paris. I had a feeling that he still had contacts with the local gendarmerie. He was a most engaging companion, and showed me how he bottled his home-grown peas, made balustrades for the garden by wrapping bandages covered in cement round iron bars, and fed his rabbits on wild rhubarb which he collected from local verges.

He suggested that collecting wild rhubarb for the rabbits would make a useful cover for my first reconnaissance of the area, on which he accompanied me, pointing out the best coastal viewpoints on the way, and showing me the Anse St Martin, where I had landed and other neighbouring features. One of these was a part of the nearby port of Omonville-la-Rogue which was the bigger and more distant of the two local harbours and we could see all this quite clearly from only a short distance along the lane behind his house. The other, and nearer as well as smaller harbour, was Port Racine, but this was not visible from the lane where we were. Port Racine is also known as St Germain-des-Vaux for some obscure reason, and this oddity caused me later some confusion.

Later M. Beauchaux guided me round the whole area, keeping always to the network of small lanes of which the one behind his garden was part. So carefully planned were these excursions that we avoided any encounters with his neighbours. I gained a good knowledge of the geography of the neighbourhood, learnt the position of the main German posts and billets, and mastered the intricacies of the little-used hill tracks. But of course I had no opportunity of testing my appearance on the local people or, more importantly, on the Germans.

Finally, with M. Beauchaux's approval I started going out on my own, and quite soon, discovered I was being followed. I was returning to the house, and just as I turned off the lane into the field behind the garden, I caught sight of two girls behind me, obviously intent on watching where I went. It was too late to change direction, so I went on, and was soon out of sight behind the tall hedge surrounding the field. Looking back through the gate, I saw the girls stop and stand there watching me. If I had just carried on they would have seen me enter the garden and have learnt where I was staying. Without hesitation, I turned my back on them, sidled up to the hedge and pretended to urinate. This had the desired effect; the girls withdrew without delay and disappeared past the gate. I did not see them again.

In spite of their natural anxieties at the possible consequences of my presence, M. and Mme Beauchaux did everything they could to make my stay with them pleasant and to make me feel at home. One day I was let loose in the kitchen and allowed to cook one of my favourite dishes, a jam omelette. I used about six eggs without considering that they might be in short supply; but, in fact, at that stage of the war, food was not too difficult in the country districts of France; my cooking was pronounced a great success and my omelettes were greatly enjoyed. In the evenings Madame would play the piano and sing French songs, explaining the slang words for my benefit. She sang extremely well—to professional standards I thought—and I guessed she had been on the stage at some time. Whenever I showed by my laughter that I was enjoying her perform-ance, she would join in and laugh too, clapping her hands and crying out "Ah! C'est rigolo. C'est très rigolo!"

The comic opera "Les Cloches de Corneville" was one of their favourites; and the song Madame liked best, because she said it reminded her of me, and because it had an English melody, was the 'Complete du Mousse' (The Sailor Boy's Songs), from "La petite Maison Grise". The chorus went:

> 'va petit mousse, où le vent te pousse,
> Où te porte le flot, le flot,
> Dans ton navire, Vogue ou chavire,
> Vogue ou chavire, jusqu'au fond des eaux.'

(Go, little sailor boy, where the wind blows you, where the waves carry you, in your boat, sail or sink until at the bottom of the sea.) The verse she liked best was:

> 'peut-être qu'une reine demandera ta main,
> peut-être qu'une baleine te mangera demain.'

(Perhaps a queen will ask your hand, perhaps tomorrow a whale will eat you.)

M. Beauchaux would always join in; once he recounted how some Italian friends had joined in the chorus, but their Italian accent had made 'Où le vent te pousse' sound like 'Où le ventre te pousse' (Where the stomach pushes you). Suiting action to the words, he stuck out his rather ample stomach and pushed his hands forward expressively, repeating the line with much emphasis of the Italian 't' at the end of vent, and roaring with laughter the while. Once I did my party piece, too, and sang 'The Diver', which had a topical maritime theme, and seemed to go down well.

We talked a lot, too, about many things, especially the stage, about which Madame spoke very knowledgeably.

She asked what I thought of the Folies Bergère and I felt rather embarrassed: it was a subject not normally discussed in mixed company in England at that time. My reply was somewhat obscure, indicating perhaps a lack of enthusiasm for the show. But Madame said that she considered it had great artistic merit and was not to be dismissed merely as entertainment for men. She spoke of the artistry of dancers moving against a background of beautiful, statuesque women, and of the magnificent staging. It was like a fine ballet, she said and gave just as much pleasure to the audience. In artistic terms, she maintained, it could be appreciated in the same way as an opera or a painting.

The idea that the revelation of women's breasts on stage was part of the artistic ethos was new to me, although of course, their revelation in a painting or sculpture has always been so regarded. Most young Englishmen at that time thought of the Folies Bergère with a nudge and a snigger. Now for the first time a basically different approach was suggested to me. I decided that next time I participated in a debate on Art, I would try it out. I resisted any speculation as to when and where that might be.

For several days in this pleasantly relaxed company I made no progress with preparations for a second escape attempt, although I did sew up a canvas boat cover which I thought could come in useful, but exactly how I was not sure. Possibly at the back of my mind I was thinking of the small fishing dinghies in the harbour at Port Racine. Soon, however, I began to grow impatient for action, and my sense of urgency was increased by mention from time to time that the Germans might still want the use of my room at short notice. Finally I made up my mind that I must leave M. and Mme Beauchaux, and that I would go to Omonville-la-Rogue, and look for another boat there.

I had not the slightest idea of how I should proceed when I got there, for I had not been able, on any of my outings, to examine the craft in the harbour from close quarters, so it

106

was a matter of trying and seeing what happened. It was essential to do so in darkness, however, and so it was evening when, after an emotional farewell (both my good friends were unable to hold back their tears), I slipped out of their cottage through the back garden. I carried my tarpaulin sack, which I had retrieved from the undergrowth in which I had hid it on landing, and which still contained some of the tinned food I had stolen in Brittany, and the waterbottles, which I had refilled.

When I reached Omonville, I dumped it a little way from the quay to enable me to move more easily round the harbour, and then, keeping in the shadows as much as possible crept towards the water's edge, feeling not a little scared, for I knew there were German sentries on top of the cliffs overlooking the harbour. I had watched them practising their shooting on seagulls during one of my daylight visits to the place. Now I felt that I was myself a conspicuous target offering them the chance of further fun.

I soon realised that there was not the slightest chance of getting a boat away from the harbour, certainly not immediately, for none were afloat, and I doubted if I could drag one down from the top of the shingle unaided. In any case the noise alone would have ruled it out. I comforted myself by knowing that I had added to my knowledge of the locality, even though it was negative, and at the first sign of dawn I beat a hasty retreat, leaving my sack where I had hidden it. Fearing to go back through the village lest I ran into German guards, I took a route along the top of the beach, hoping at the same time to extend my knowledge of this section of the coastline nearby, which I had not previously explored, as it was not accessible from the hill tracks that I had kept to. Unfortunately the path I chose led straight into a marsh, and although I followed an upward course which I thought would lead to drier ground, the higher I went the deeper I sank into the bog. It must have been at least an hour before I found firm footing; but at last I got clear, and then (for I had no alternative) I made my way back to the safety of the house which I had so recently left.

I slipped into my bed with mixed feelings; wondering what my reception would be but greatly relieved that my room had not been given to a German. I luxuriated in the pleasure of lying once more in a soft real bed and congratulated myself on having escaped detection on the way, in the morning light. And my fears that my reappearance might be unwelcome were dispelled as soon as I woke. Both my friends were overjoyed to see me again, Mme Beauchaux telling me that her husband had wept after I had gone, and prayed for me long into the night.

All the same, I felt rather foolish about my abortive escape attempt; I made up my mind to try again without delay. This time I determined to make a better job of it and decided to go to the much smaller harbour at Port Racine, which I had heard described as the smallest harbour in France. I had already seen the boats there from a distance, and from what I had observed of the way they were moored, thought there was a chance that I might find one at least, if not more, afloat.

I set out again that evening, my second parting as emotional as the first, and reached Port Racine without difficulty. But once more I found that there was no chance of taking a boat immediately. There were five moored in the harbour, but two were no more than cockleshells—they looked in fact home-made. And two out of the other three, both fair-sized fishing smacks, one afloat and the other beached, were unrigged and had no sails aboard. The fifth vessel was a small motor boat, but I did not give serious thought to the idea of using it: I had no way of obtaining petrol, and if I did, the noise of the engine would surely be an instant give-away. In any case, it was on the small side for crossing the Channel, about fifteen feet long and only quarter-decked.

However, I had resolved not to return a second time to

the Beauchaux, so I looked for somewhere near the harbour to sleep, and found a small stone hut at the side of a footpath not far from the jetty. It was crude and dirty, but it offered an excellent view of the coast road, the harbour, and the ten or twelve cottages that made up the village. And it was empty. I spent the night undisturbed in it; and in the morning I accepted the conclusion I had been considering during the night, that I must abandon any further attempt to keep my existence secret, although still with an open mind as to my story if confronted.

With no attempt at concealment, therefore, I wandered next day round the harbour, along the coast road, and out on to the headland of the Anse St Martin to the west of the bay. At the very tip of the headland I found a Napoleonic Fort, which despite its age was in excellent condition; it appeared deserted, so I slipped in through a window and methodically went through it. The place was fully furnished, with beds and bedding, a kitchen properly equipped and a comprehensive medicine cupboard. There were books too, and, of the greatest value to me, maps and charts of the local coast. And in one room I found a roll of canvas of the type used for sailmaking; there was cotton thread as well, but not a needle anywhere.

I decided to move into the fort at once, and to start work on making a sail as soon as I had a needle. I walked back to the village in the hope of getting one, and seeing an old woman outside a cottage by the quay, asked her if I could borrow one from her; I racked my brains all the way in an effort to recall the French word 'aiguille' and succeeded just in time. She nodded assent and asking no questions, though I could see she was bursting with curiosity, went into her cottage to fetch one which she handed to me; by chance or design it was of a suitably masculine size. I returned at once to the fort with it and set to work without delay stitching canvas steadily for most of the remainder of the day. By evening I had almost half completed a sail that I hoped might fit the fishing smack which was afloat in the harbour. I congratulated myself on what I considered to be excellent needlework and the sail was beginning to take shape and looking quite neat. Once or twice I took a break, and each time examined in detail a different section of the immediate surroundings.

There was of course a danger that German troops might turn up at any moment, for the fort was in a strategic position on the coast; but I had found no signs of vehicle tracks in the vicinity, and reckoned that it should be safe to stay in the place at least one night, encouraged possibly by the idea of sleeping once more in a comfortable bed. I suffered only one shock when suddenly confronted by a motionless owl perched on a tree outside. It did not stir when I approached it, and I left it in peace, thinking its presence confirmed that the fort was unused.

In case I was caught in the night, however, I worked out an escape plan. There were two entrances, one at ground level which opened on to the bottom of what I took to be a dried out moat, and the other on the first floor, opening on to a footbridge which spanned the moat. Whichever entrance any intruders might use, I planned to slip out unseen by the other. The plan, of course, had a weakness: it would not work if both entrances were used simultaneously: but I thought the Germans, who were in a very confident and relaxed mood, were unlikely to take elaborate precautions, if they came at all. I was also counting on not being taken unawares, particularly while asleep.

I fetched my tarpaulin sack, and had some of the food provided by Mme Beauchaux; and then I enjoyed another undisturbed night in most civilised comfort. Next morning, I went out again, and while engaged on some more local reconnaissance, encountered an old fisherman, who turned out to be the husband of the lady who had lent me the needle. After being with him for a short while, I gained the feeling that he was a man who could be trusted, and, perhaps rashly, told him something of my story and why I had wanted the needle. He made no immediate comment, and presently I returned to the fort and work on the sail. I was busy in one of the lower rooms with the sail when I heard footsteps, and then voices. They were in the room above me, from which the upper door of the fort opened on to the bridge. I quickly gathered the still unfinished sail into a bundle, and ran out of the building through the lower door, crossed the moat, and emerged on to a narrow path along the cliff. As I did so, I saw the old fisherman, and my first thought was that he had betrayed me to the Gestapo: my suspicions seemed confirmed when, as soon as I appeared, he turned and fled. I dumped the sail in some bushes and ran after him, angrily shouting, "Stop!" I soon overhauled him, and demanded to know what he was up to, virtually accusing him of betraying me. "No no," he replied, pointing to the fort, "I have brought a friend to you, who wants to help you."

At that moment the friend, who had heard the shouting, came along the path and joined us; and a very useful friend he promised to be. His name was Manime, and within a short time he took over responsibility for all my problems as if he had been appointed my manager. He said that he would secure a boat, and everything else I needed to make my escape to England, but that meanwhile I should not remain another hour in the fort, for the Germans might take it over at any minute. Thinking that all my troubles were over, I readily agreed to return at once to the stone hut by the jetty.

From there, M. Manime said, I should go to a nearby farm which belonged to a cousin of his, and where he would arrange a job for me while he organised a boat. Although I pressed him to tell me what sort of boat he had in mind, he would only say a good big one, "quite capable of crossing the Channel". It turned out that he owned the motor boat I had seen in the harbour, but the idea of using it did not register with me at the time, no doubt because of the danger of its noise being heard, as well as the problem of petrol.

For the next day or two I saw him; he brought soused mackerel in a biscuit tin as a dish, bread, and a bottle of wine to the stone hut to keep me going while he fixed things with his cousin. Meanwhile I continued with making exhaustive surveys of the coast, chiefly westwards from the harbour and in the direction of the Cap de la Hague. I soon realised there was little chance of finding a boat there, for there were high cliffs all the way along, except for one small gap, at the outermost point of the cape, where there was a fishing harbour, facing Alderney. From the cliffs above the harbour the Blanchart Race was clearly visible, and the sight of its distinctive line of white foam brought back such painful memories to me that I turned away with a feeling of revulsion, and resolved that under no circumstances would I attempt to start another voyage from anywhere near it.

I saw several parties of German troops about in the village of the harbour, chiefly Luftwaffe personnel, and once, while I was prowling round the outskirts, saw a party of officers going in to lunch at a little hotel overlooking the straits. On either side of the harbour, high up on the cliff edge, I could see gun detachments equipped with mobile 2-pounder type guns.

Returning to Port Racine, I continued to make no attempt to hide away but hung about the jetty and the nearby beach near my stone hut, talking to the local fishermen and village boys as they cleaned and dried their nets; one of the fishermen was Mangepin, had seen me sail into the bay St Martin. Sometimes I lent them a hand, and in this way I got to know most of the village people, including some of the children; I became friendly with two boys in particular, spending many hours idly talking with them, sometimes watching the Germans bathing or doing PT exercises which they took very seriously.

I was sitting talking to the boys one day when a fat

112

German officer approached and addressed us. He was wearing grey lisle cotton gloves of which he seemed inordinately proud, and as he spoke he gestured with his hands like a ballet dancer. First he talked of the tide and asked when it would be high; and then he went on to enquire about the possibility of hiring a boat, seemingly directing his question to me as being the eldest. I could tell him the time of the high tide, but not about a boat. I said he would have to ask the owner—'le patron'. Then he announced that he wanted a crab; I asked him how big did he want it and a little demonstration with his hands followed. I said I would see what I could do, but warned him that crabs were scarce, and we did not get many. With that he went his way, suspecting I felt sure, that his leg had been pulled. Fortunately I did not see him again. The meeting, however, had given me a useful opportunity of testing my ability to pass as a Frenchman under German scrutiny in a relatively stable situation, as I had done earlier in near-battle conditions.

After a few days, M. Manime took me to his cousin's farm, advising me on the way not to do anything in a hurry, but to stay quietly at the farm for the present. Major developments were expected, he said, and there might be no need for an escape attempt at all. I presumed that he was anticipating a German invasion of England and perhaps Britain's surrender. At any rate, it seemed to me that his attitude had changed alarmingly, and that he was no longer very keen to help me. But when I accused him of losing interest in helping me he assured me that this was not so: he would keep his promise and find a boat for me in six or seven days. So I relaxed once more and looked ahead with pleasure to a week of good food and open-air exercise.

When we arrived at the farm I was at once presented to Mme Gemmetel, the farmer's wife, who gave me a friendly welcome, and said that although I should be working as a farm labourer, I would be treated as one of the family, and sit with them for meals; not at the separate table used by the farm workers—the 'domestiques'—whose fare was of a lower standard. This consisted, I found, mainly of 'soupe', made from vegetables, principally cabbage, and a meat extract called 'graisse' (also known as graisse Normandaise), which was followed by bread and dripping and accompanied by cider to drink. The family had some extras, such as hot bread and milk at 6 o'clock breakfast, and a meat course at the midday meal.

I found the routine of farm life pleasant; up at 5.30 a.m. for half an hour's work before breakfast; then hot bread and milk and coffee. On fine days we four field labourers would then collect our 'collation' of bread, pork dripping and a bottle of cider each and go out again to work. On wet days we worked in the timber shed, cutting up tree trunks, first splitting them with wedges and then sawing them into log lengths. Halfway through the morning we would take a break for our collation, and at midday we would return to the farm for lunch. After lunch we collected an identical collation for the afternoon; and we finally returned to the farm for our evening meal between 6 and 7 o'clock. After the meal we had coffee, and occasionally a Calvados 'fine', a spirit distilled from cider; and then it was straight to bed, for which I was always quite ready. It was a healthy life and after a few days I felt as fit as ever, cutting rye and barley with a scythe, hoeing cabbage, carrots and dwarf beans, and at the end of the week helping to get in the hay.

I had always imagined haymaking as the easiest job on a farm, but in practice I found it the most strenuous of all, and sprained my wrist at it. Mme Gemmetel expressed much concern (she called it 'surpoigné'), dressed it with liniment, and wrapped it round with a bandage. But then she immediately asked me to carry a heavy copper full of water from the house to a stream which ran nearby! Despite that little inconsistency, she was a vivacious and very likeable person, typically French, I thought. She worried about my French

114

accent, which she said gave me away every time I opened my mouth, which she pointed out was too wide. She took a lot of trouble correcting my pronunciation. When speaking keep your teeth closed and use only your lips to form the sounds. In this way you avoid the typical English fault of saying 'Boco' instead of beaucoup. She drummed this lesson into me as well as others and I felt very pleased that I could now almost pass as a Frenchman as a result. Up till then the other workers had been told that I spoke the way I did because I came from the north, but that I was a relation. This also explained my sitting at the family table. The farmer's boy, however, I suspected, had an idea I was English, because he was constantly talking about the stories of British parachutists which were the subject of local rumours. I felt sorry for him, for he was endlessly chased by everyone and seemed to live a dog's life.

Sometimes I was sent out alone on errands or to work in the fields on weeding jobs with the boy. Such occasions gave me a chance to explore surreptitiously the neighbourhood. They also provided opportunities for casual conversation with German soldiers on sentry duty in the area. On one occasion the boy prompted me to ask the time in German of one of the sentries. Some of the rumours about my activities that I learnt of afterwards must have emanated I think, on looking back, from the boy, especially about the risks I took in talking to the Germans. On another occasion, this time when I was on my own, I was walking along a road some way from the farm (movement was not restricted in daytime, only at night after curfew), when a German army car stopped and the driver asked if I would like a lift. I thought it politic to accept, for there were no houses in the immediate vicinity, and it was obvious that I must have a long walk ahead of me. I asked him to take me to the next village, where I said I was visiting a friend. The driver probably hoped to be invited in with me when we arrived, but I made it clear that I was not going to my own home and thought therefore that I could reasonably thank him and say goodbye at the gate.

When I got back to the farm, I found Mme Gemmetel in a great state; she said she had been looking everywhere for me. I thought she must be annoyed with me for disappearing without telling anyone where I was going, or perhaps that I had been seen getting into a German car and that this had alarmed her. Whatever the truth of the matter, however, all she asked me to do was to help her catch a goose they were going to have for dinner.

I was a complete failure at goose catching as she must have known quite well, and she had to get the farmer's boy to show me how to go about it. He could indeed have done the job in the first place. When we finally caught the bird, Mme Gemmetel bent its head back and sliced across the back of its neck until the blood started to flow out, to be collected in a basin and later used to make gravy. After a few minutes the goose collapsed, and mercifully died. The episode sounds revolting, but it was I imagine a normal part of farm life, though I did not rule out the possibility that Madame might have chosen it as a demonstration to me of the error of straying off the farm and accepting lifts from Germans.

Another odd job in which I was involved was the ringing of a young bull. This was done by inserting a metal ring, rather like a large key ring with overlapping layers, into the cartilage between its nostrils. When done—and it was quite a job—a rope was tied to the ring, and the bull was led out to grass. On the day after my haymaking accident it rained and I was told to saw up some timber; M. Gemmetel came into the shed where I was working and noticed that I was only using one hand on a double-ended saw. He made some critical comment about the slack way I was holding the saw, and asked why I wasn't using both hands. I explained that I could not use the other hand owing to the sprain, hoping that his wife would hear about it in due course, and possibly have cause for thought.

M. Manime who had got me the job on the farm was, I discovered, a dentist with a practice in Cherbourg. His connection with M. Gemmetel, the farmer, was through Mme Manime, who came to the farm one day while I was again cutting wood. Accompanied by Mme Gemmetel, she came out to see me. She had a parcel in her arms, and handed it to me with a gracious smile, saying that it was a present. Inside I found a clean shirt which I was very pleased to have. But the gift made me wonder what Mme Gemmetel must have thought of the one I was wearing. Was the present, perhaps, a diplomatic way which she had thought up of getting me to change it?

I had enjoyed this idyllic existence on the farm for about a week when it was rudely interrupted by the arrival of a party of German soldiers. Keeping carefully in the background, but within earshot, I was half relieved, half dismayed to learn that they had come, not to pick up an escaped POW, but to be billeted on this comfortable farm.

ELEVEN

Growing Despair

There were ten or twelve German soldiers in the party, and their arrival did not really alarm me as much as it did Mme Gemmetel. Her husband showed no outward sign of concern, although in the light of later events I think he must have been as alarmed as she was. She told me not to speak in the Germans' presence, and if addressed by them, to be particularly careful with my accent when replying. In fact they frequently talked to me, and I did nothing to discourage them; I hoped that I might learn something of the local German troop movements, of preparations for the invasion of England, and of the progress of the war generally. Just how near this was to espionage I did not stop to debate: it seemed good sense to make the most of having enemy troops at such close quarters.

I had once toyed with the idea of masquerading as a German soldier, after being asked the way by a despatch rider near Boursies, and as I had not completely dismissed it from my mind, I made it a practice to take advantage of every opportunity that came my way to practise speaking and conversing in German. By now I was quite at ease in the company of ordinary German soldiers, most of who seemed to be simple enough, although I was not so sure about the NCO's, and definitely wary of their officers. As a result I was able to help them frequently if they could not make themselves understood by the farm people and soon I was the accepted interpreter when language difficulties arose, even for the farmer's wife.

After a while I became a little careless. One day a soldier wanted to send a parcel home, and asked for paper and string with which to wrap it. Madame could not understand him, and they both turned to me for assistance. Proud of my vocabulary I obliged at once, saying he wanted, "du papier et ficelle". Leaving Madame to fetch the materials the soldier went out of the room, saying as he did, "Komm gleich". I turned to Madame, and translated his words into English, "He'll soon be back." She looked at me in horror; several other soldiers were present as well as some farm workers. A little impatient at her obtuseness, I repeated again in English, "He's coming back in a minute". The look of horror on Mme Gemmetel's face intensified, and at last I came to my senses, realising what I had done. I covered up my blunder as quickly as possible with: "Ah. Pardon. C'est Flamand. Il dit qu'il reviendra toute suite". (Sorry. That was Flemish. He said he'll be back at once). The atmosphere relaxed, but I shuddered as I thought of the possible consequences of my carelessness, and pledged myself to be more circumspect in future.

In fact, I got little information from the Germans: all they would say was that their next move was to England. They never tired of announcing that England was 'Kaput', and in the process of being pulverised out of existence. I struck up a sort of camaraderie with one old sweat who'd seen service in the First World War, and who seemed to me to be the only normal human being among them; his failing was the bottle, which constantly got him into trouble. Before coming to the farm, he had done three days in the German 'glasshouse' at Cherbourg for insolence to an officer. He seemed none the worse for it, and entertained us with descriptions of how he had been punished. He said that he had been strapped to a chair (demonstrating to us how he had been positioned) in a cellar, and left in it for the whole three days of his sentence with rats running all over him. Whether he was pulling our legs or not I could not tell; but we listened with rapt attention to his story, and he clearly enjoyed telling it.

The other soldiers were young Nazis who took themselves and the war very seriously, and were conscious all the time of their position as conquerors. Occasionally, after the evening meal, which they took separately in their own room, some of them would come in and join the family for coffee and Calvados, always behaving very correctly. One evening one of the farm workers asked when they thought the war would end. A sudden hush descended on the room: after a few seconds one of the soldiers rose to his feet and stood rigidly to attention. Then, as if addressing a public meeting, he replied: "There is only one who knows when the war will end—and that is Herr Hitler. Heil Hitler." After which he gave the Nazi salute as stiffly as if on parade, and sat down. I had to make an effort to restrain my laughter.

Later the same evening, my guard weakened by the jovial atmosphere (and the Calvados), I forgot caution and nearly gave myself away again. I was talking to Fritz, the old sweat, and he asked me what I did in peacetime. I told him I had been a sailor, and we started talking about the sea. I had become so accustomed to changing my background to fit the occasion that I began to elaborate about my life rather more than was strictly necessary; Fritz (that really was his name) asked me where I had sailed, and I replied I'd visited South Africa, and Norway and lots of places in between, none of which in reality I had ever been near. Then he asked me if I knew Rotterdam, and thinking he might have just come from the city, which the Germans had only recently captured, I said that I didn't know it, but that I had been to Hamburg and Bremen on one voyage. As soon as I mentioned Hamburg, his eyes lit up; looking at me intently, albeit with a smile, he stuck his finger out at me and said "Ach! Englander! Du bist Englander! Ja?"

It was the way I had pronounced Hamburg that gave me away. I had said 'Hamburg' instead of 'Humbooorch'. Of course I denied it strenuously, and repeated the story which had served me so well before, that I came from the north of France, and that my mother was Flemish. I was sure though that Fritz had rumbled me, and I often wonder whether, if I had admitted being English, he would have given me away. I guess that the chances are fifty-fifty that he would not, for it was obvious that he had no love for the Nazis. However that may be, at any rate, he did not refer to it again, and we both seemed to accept that we had some sort of secret understanding.

Any chance of developing the relationship further was ruled out however by movement orders which came next day for about half of the party, Fritz among them. Before leaving, the Germans told us, in strict confidence, that their destination was England, but I heard later that they had gone to a place on the coast on the other side of Cherbourg. They held a party in their room, which lasted till the small hours, the night before their departure; everyone got more than merry, two chairs were broken, and Madame was furious. She went off first thing in the morning to the Kommandatur headquarters to lodge a complaint. It was official German policy at that time to take special care to maintain good relations with the civilian population, and that evening a very worried, nervous looking German corporal arrived at the farm by bicycle to apologise for the trouble and pay for the damage.

Soon after this, rumours began to circulate in the Port Racine area of German corpses being washed ashore, some having apparently been burnt; and it was also reported that German troops had refused to embark for the invasion of England, and had been marched away under arrest, while others had been shot for refusing to obey orders, and their bodies burnt in a special cremating machine. There were stories too of shootings and rape in neighbouring villages; but I never saw any evidence of either myself, or heard of anyone who knew the alleged victims.

I did, however, figure in one of the rumours, as a mysterious Englishman, known as 'L'Anglais', who was engaged in secret intelligence work, and allegedly active all over the district. People who knew me began to believe the story; when I passed them on the road they would avert their eyes from me. Mme Manime was one who never acknowledged me in public, although she had been formally introduced to me, and she had given me the shirt I was wearing.

M. Manime, meanwhile, was getting vaguer and vaguer about the boat he had promised to secure for me, and I began again to have serious doubts about his reliability. I suspected that he was deliberately avoiding me, for he entirely ceased coming to the farm, although earlier he had been a frequent visitor. Although he had his dentist's practice in Cherbourg, he lived near Port Racine in quite a large house.

One evening, having heard nothing for several days about what he was supposed to be doing for me, I went to see him at his home, even though I realised that he might not be very happy at my appearing there. Fortunately, I found him in, and at once asked him point blank whether he was doing anything about the boat, and if so, when I could expect to have some news about it. He looked me unblinkingly straight in the eye, and replied that since he last spoke to me about it the situation had changed and become much more dangerous, so much so that it was no longer possible for him to obtain a boat. Too many village people suspected him of helping me, he went on, and if we were not careful we would both be arrested and shot. The only thing for me to do was to go south into the unoccupied part of France, and try from there to get into Spain.

I was bitter and furious at what I saw as his blatant betrayal of his promises, and shouted at him in my atrocious French: "Vous m'avez perdu mon temps!", by which I intended to mean he had been wasting my time. I did not wait to see whether he had got the message. I just wheeled round and stumped off out of his garden where we had been standing by the gate. I had not, of course, taken into account the tense atmosphere which had developed in the last few days as the war with England continued and threatened to grow more and more bitter. Nor indeed did I consider the risks incurred by anyone helping an escaped British soldier, the more so in M. Manime's case as he was the owner of a boat and accordingly subject to close attention by both the French gendarmerie and the German authorities, particularly with the activities, real or rumoured, of a sea-borne invasion of England. To be fair to him, there was absolutely no obligation on his part to assist me; it was just that he had raised my hopes.

I returned to the farm with a heavy heart, all my hopes of getting home shattered yet again. Mme Gemmetel tried to cheer me up, after I told her the bad news that there was no hope of a boat; that I would have to give up trying, and make instead for the south and Spain. As we talked I mentioned to her that I had heard some of the fishermen in Cherbourg were sailing occasionally to the British Isles. Some stories even said they were carrying German soldiers there. I said I couldn't really believe them and had not taken them seriously; but Madame thought it worth trying to find out more and said it might be worth my seeing a friend of hers, a M. Mauler, who was in the wholesale fish trade, a 'morayeur', in Cherbourg, and as he was in almost daily contact with the fishing boat captains, would know what was really going on. He was very pro-British, she added, and if I mentioned her name would do all he could to help me.

Glad to clutch at any straw, I said I would go to see him next day, whereupon Madame gave me exact instructions about how to get to Cherbourg by the bus that did the round of the villages on the Cap de la Hague every morning. The nearest stopping place to the farm was at Omonville-la-Petite where I should board it. She also told me the fare, and made sure that I had the exact amount in small change so that I would not attract attention.

Next morning I was at the bus stop in good time and joined three or four housewives already there, who looked as if they were going in to Cherbourg shopping. After ten minutes or so the bus arrived, and I followed them aboard, found a vacant seat and got my ticket without difficulty, saying only "Cherbourg" when the conductor came round. He was just as monosyllabic, and did not give me a second glance.

The bus made a circuit of the Cape before setting off for Cherbourg. One of the villages it stopped at was Digulleville and who should get in but Mme Beauchaux who had befriended me when I first landed, with the fine pair of trousers I was still wearing. She looked at me as though she had seen a ghost, and then immediately turned away, giving no sign of recognition. By now I was used to being ignored in public, and also looked quickly away. Soon after leaving Digulleville the bus filled up, and I lost sight of her. And when I got out at the harbour at Cherbourg, she had disappeared.

The Cherbourg fish merchants were not difficult to find; they all seemed to be located in a group on the quayside, each shop having a storage yard adjoining. I soon saw M. Mauler's name painted in big letters over a large double-fronted shop with a spacious forecourt, on which baskets of fish of all kinds were displayed. I walked round the courtyard examining the fish as if I were a prospective customer, and soon identified M. Mauler, a pleasant looking man in fishmonger's overalls. He was talking and joking with a buyer and I waited until he was free before approaching him. Then I asked if I was speaking to M. Mauler, and on learning that I was, explained that Mme Gemmetel had given me his name as being a friend who might be able to help me. Could he spare a few minutes, please?

Before replying he went out on to the pavement, looking both ways to see that it was clear of any one suspicious, and as I followed him to the curb, our conversation got under way as if we were two fish dealers bargaining. When I explained my problem to him he replied that the rumour I had heard about fishermen ferrying German soldiers was partly true, but that the Isles to which they went were the Channel Islands and not the British mainland. General cargo, including stores for the German occupation troops was taken out and tomatoes brought back. And troops of the occupation forces were ferried in and out at the same time. It was, however, out of the question to think that I could get a boat to take me to England; none of the fishermen would be prepared even to consider the idea. M. Mauler added that in his opinion it would be plain suicide to try to sail to England, and I would be well advised to forget the whole idea.

While we were talking, M. Manime, the dentist, came along the street, and stopped when he saw me. He did not seem to bear any resentment at my behaviour of the previous day, but greeted me in a friendly way and invited me to go to his surgery, which was nearby. He seemed anxious to restore good relations, so I accepted the invitation and decided to apologise for my bad temper. Since my funds were running low I thought it a good idea to tell him I had decided to take his advice and head for Spain, but if I did so I should need cash and this might be a good chance to ask if he could help. I was indeed beginning to think that I might be forced to go south after all.

M. Manime told me to follow him, adding that we should not talk until we were in his office and he had given me the all clear. We walked to a building not far from the fish quay, went through an imposing entrance, and climbed the stairs to the second floor, where he had his practice; as we passed through an outer office M. Manime told his receptionist that we were not to be disturbed on any account, and entered his surgery.

As soon as the door closed, he went across to the dentist's chair and switched on the drill. Then, holding it in his hand, he said it was safe to talk. He asked if I had any news, and what my plans were, and I explained why I had come to see the fish merchant. It now seemed clear, I went on, that there was no hope of getting a boat to take me to England, and that I should have to change my plans and go south to Spain. There were two major difficulties however: I had no bicycle and very little money.

He was non-committal about helping me, but more interested in discussing the best route for me to take to the south. He advised me to make for the unoccupied zone, going inland, then continuing south to Coutances, to Laval, then southeast to Poitiers, and from there continuing due south towards the Spanish border. I felt sure that he did not know what conditions were like in the unoccupied zone; and it became obvious that he was not going to give me the names of any contacts to help me on my way, and, most important of all, to assist me to get across the frontier into Spain.

Once again, I thought, I was wasting my time with him; but before I left, I asked him directly if he himself owned a motor boat. He answered that indeed he did, and without more ado I asked if it would be possible for me to borrow it, on the understanding that it would be returned to him after the war, in good condition, any damage fully repaired or paid for. He forebore from any scepticism on the worth of such an undertaking but said firmly that it was absolutely out of the question; the boat was at Port Racine, and the German commander there had already told him that he or members of his staff would be using it, and that it must be kept in a state of constant readiness. He added that in any case he only had a small supply of petrol left, quite insufficient for crossing the Channel, and that there was no way of getting any more. I realised that I was in danger of making myself an unwelcome embarrassment from which he could all too easily free himself by a hint in the right quarter, so I thanked him for his courtesy, saying I had to catch my bus home, and left his surgery, looking as sorry for myself as if the drill had in fact been painfully active.

The bus did not leave until much later in the afternoon, which gave me a chance to have a look round Cherbourg, which I thought could be useful while it was relatively free from restriction. I made my way along the fish quay towards the main harbour, noticing that there were plenty of people out on the streets, but very little traffic. Quite soon I saw a party of British prisoners marching towards the docks, no doubt to work there. It seemed odd to be standing by without making myself known but there was no profit in adding to their numbers. Their cheerfulness and good spirits was impressive, and so was their marching, which I thought compared very favourably with that of a German contingent shambling the opposite way, exuding gloom and despondency. It may of course have been a forced labour gang from one of the conquered territories, in which case its luckless members had good cause for looking miserable.

People lined the pavement, three deep in places,

watching in complete silence, as the detachment, thirty or forty strong, strode along the middle of the street. I followed in the same direction after they had passed and presently came to another quay which ran one side of an open square. In the square was an attractive café-restaurant, the Café de Paris, which was obviously popular both with the local people and the Germans; and on the spur of the moment I decided to go in and indulge in a special treat to cheer myself up after the disappointment of the morning events. I secured a table near the window, from which I could watch customers coming in and going out—and found it an entertainment in itself. The French mostly gave an impression of well-behaved reserve, bordering on humility, and were extremely quiet and careful as they came in, while the Germans, mainly officers, swaggered in in twos and threes, and took their seats in a slap-dash, careless and bored manner, saluting with a per-functory wave of the hand and wrist and a brief "L'itler" of which nobody took any notice. I was very relieved that none of the Germans took any interest in me, although I really felt there was no reason for them to do so; I had got so accustomed to thinking of myself as a Frenchman, despite my abortive attempts to reach England. Certainly the waitresses gave me some queer looks, clearly wondering where I fitted in, but I had no problems in ordering the meal; they were no doubt used to foreign visitors and my accent caused no comment. The lunch was first class, and I felt a new man after it, my bleak prospects temporarily forgotten. I just hoped it would be the last call on my near-empty purse.

The bus home was packed; I only just managed to squeeze in, and had to stand most of the way. Mme Beauchaux was in a seat on the opposite side of the gangway. When I first saw her we exchanged a fleeting glance, but otherwise again gave no sign of recognition. I got a surly look from the conductor when I asked for a ticket to Omonville, the reason only becoming clear when we reached Omonville-la-Rogue. This is a more important place than Omonville-la-Petite and clearly he assumed it to be the destination of anyone who did not specify otherwise. When I did not get out there, he came up and demanded to know why. After some difficult explanations I managed to persuade him to accept the extra fare due, although he took it with a bad grace, obviously thinking I had been trying to cheat the bus company. Fortunately not many people were left on board by this time, and his grumblings were mostly unheard. I adopted a meek and ingratiating manner, but this appeared only to annoy him the more and it was some time before he gave up muttering and complaining.

A French army officer, who had obviously just been released from imprisonment, was on the bus with his wife, and I felt a pang of envy as I saw their happiness; only to be followed almost immediately by a feeling of pity, for I was sure it could only be short-lived. When we finally reached Omonville-la-Petite, I felt the conductor's disapproving eyes on me as I alighted and was prepared for another round of denunciations. Mercifully, however, he said nothing, and I made my way as fast as I could to the farm, glad to have seen the last of him.

As I walked from the bus-stop, my spirits again sank and I felt as depressed as I had before lunch. I racked my brains without success for a way out of what seemed increasingly a hopeless situation, and by the time I reached the farm was feeling really desperate once more. I decided that I must move out, and try my luck on the shore. Fortunate as I had been in all my encounters, friends or enemies, I had no wish to get used to this kind of existence. I desperately needed to get back to the job I had undertaken, and to do that I knew I must tackle the sea.

As soon as she saw me, Mme Gemmetel asked how I had got on; I told her what M. Manime had said, and she realised from the tone of my reply that I was in complete despair. She had spoken several times before of the help that comes from prayer in times of trouble, especially through the communion of saints, and now she said that she would pray for me, and that I should pray with her, in particular to Our Lady of Lourdes and the Blessed Theresa of Lisieux. She asked me to kneel with her, and repeat after her some of the prayers she said.

I did as she asked; but when we rose, I told her that I had made up my mind to leave the farm that night, and that I would make another attempt to get a boat myself. She did not try to dissuade me, but gave me a meal, and soon after I said goodbye to her and her husband and thanked them for all they had done for me. Before I left she insisted on giving me a medallion of Our Lady of Lourdes, and as she pinned it on my shirt she told me that I should not hesitate to call on Our Lady for assistance if I was ever in danger. Her burning faith was good to see in her war-dismembered country and at a time of such disillusion, and at least in part I found myself sharing it.

I had a feeling that both she and her husband were relieved at my departure, although neither of them had ever implied that I was no longer welcome. The introduction of a registration scheme for all adult males had been announced, however, and the gendarmes had already started checking up on the farm labourers in the area.

I had been keeping my eyes open for likely looking hide-outs all the time I was at the farm, and had identified two possible locations. One was a cart-shed directly overlooking the coast road, with a loft above, dry and well provided with straw and a rear exit straight on to the hillside behind. The other was a stone hut about two miles inland up in the hills, which was used by shepherds in the lambing season. The hut was too far away to reach that night, but the cart shed on the coast road was reasonably near and it proved a comfortable refuge. I had a good night's sleep in the loft amongst the hay, and in the morning decided to stay on there awhile.

It afforded a good view of the coast road, from which I could monitor the passing traffic, so that after two or three days I had a good knowledge of the pattern of local German troop movements, which I found was regular and predictable. Despite the curfew, after a night or two I began to go out after dark, staying on deserted country lanes at first, and then, with increasing confidence, going down to the coast and prowling around the harbour, not returning till the early hours of the morning.

I soon learnt the exact positions of the various guard points, and how to detour safely round them; the sentries could nearly always be heard stamping their boots to warm their feet well before they were in sight, and apart from them, there were few Germans about at night. The occasional army truck or staff car could always be heard, and its lights seen, in time to hide behind a hedge or wall before it passed. There were, it is true, occasional revellers returning to base, but they always gave plenty of warning of their approach, and I came to regard them as a sort of comic relief; they caused me no worry at all.

What did sometimes create difficulties for me was the dropping of flares by aircraft. I did not think that the Germans would want to light up the countryside in this way—they certainly did not appear to make any use of the illumination provided. I could only assume that the flares were dropped by British planes on reconnaissance. I felt a little annoyed with the RAF, if that was correct, for interfering with my freedom of movement, for after any flares were dropped I had to lie low for quite a long time until they had burned out.

Although I stayed in the cart shed throughout the daylight hours, and discontinued all contact with the local people, my nightly excursions kept me informed about the condition and movement of the craft in the harbour at Port Racine, and I kept myself ready to take advantage of any favourable developments which might take place, such as the appearance of sails on any of the fishing boats, or signs of any deliveries of petrol that I could gain access to. Sadly, however, there were none, and presently I began to spend more of my time exploring the hills behind the port and village.

After a few days my water supplies began to run low, which was a nuisance, for the only way I could replenish them was by carrying empty bottles to the farm at night and filling them at the standpipe in the yard, a laborious and time-wasting chore. One day, however, on a trip into the hills, I discovered a pleasant, clear little stream not far from the shepherd's hut which I had previously marked down as a possible retreat, and this decided me to move there at once. It was an idyllic spot, high and remote, to which no one seemed to come, and I felt a great sense of security as I was installed in it. There followed perhaps the pleasantest interlude of all my days on the run. Each morning I shaved by a pool formed over the gravel bed of the stream which was so clear that my face was reflected as if by a mirror. No longer feeling it was unsafe to go out in daylight, I soon began to move about quite freely, using small footpaths which did not appear to be frequented at all and in this way exploring a large area of the surrounding district. I even penetrated as far as the farm where I had been working, and occasionally visiting the Gemmetels for a quick meal, or to obtain bread and other necessities. On these occasions I did not go into the farmhouse; if the coast was clear I would knock at the back door, quickly whisper what I needed and leave without delay. Hiding in a nearby hedge a short way down the farm road, I would then wait until Madame or M. Gemmetel brought out what I had requested. They never refused me.

I was able to reduce my demands on them by reverting to my former practice of breaking into deserted houses. In one

I made a good haul of tinned food which had clearly been hoarded; and to my delight also found a modest wine store in the same house. On a second visit, however, I suffered a disappointment: the remaining wine had gone, and as I left, by the same window through which I had entered I was not altogether surprised to see a man at a nearby farm watching me suspiciously. He made no attempt to follow me but disappeared in the opposite direction. I came to the only possible conclusion—he was on his way to inform the gendarmes.

Meanwhile nothing changed in the harbour, the state of the boats remaining the same, and my spirits sank steadily. Each time I visited the Gemmetels they seemed a little more nervous, and I became convinced that they knew more about plans to register the local population than they told me. I did learn, however, that the new identity cards were expected to be issued soon. I knew that when that happened it would be only a matter of time before the gendarmes were on to me. I now began to get seriously worried, feeling all the time I was being driven further and further into a corner, with the sea so near but seemingly inaccessible.

One morning I sat brooding in the shepherd's hut, too depressed even to go to the stream to shave. Dismally I considered the various possibilities open to me, dismissed most of them, and tried to come to terms with what seemed the only remaining option I could take: abandon the sea, pack up and make for the south. That way, I knew, I would encounter new dangers, not the least being that in the unoccupied zone I would have to deal with Vichy French officials who would know after I'd spoken half a dozen words that I was English. Moreover, I now had no bicycle, and even if I secured one, I was sure that movement across France would be far more difficult than it had been when I made my way from the north to Brittany: for one thing, I had no identity papers, which would soon be legally required, and for another, the gendarmes would be warned about me in advance. I was in a mood of complete despair, and then I remembered the medallion of Notre Dame de Lourdes which Mme Gemmetel had given me and on impulse, took it out of my pocket, offered up a silent prayer, and as I finished praying, kissed it.

Then everything seemed to happen at once. After only a few minutes, there was a loud banging on the door of the hut and looking through the window, I saw Mangepin, the fisherman who had seen me sail into the bay in such a pathetic manner and stagger ashore after that first shattering attempt. I let him in, and in a state of great excitement he told me that the gendarmes had found my hiding place and even now were on their way to arrest me. I must follow him without a moment's delay, and he would show me a safe hiding place. Then he would help to find a boat and get away.

The news of danger and the need for action released a lot of pent-up energy in me; quickly I collected what belongings I could and then left the hut, following a short distance behind Mangepin, who had gone on ahead and kept calling back to me, "Vite. Vite. Venez. Venez. Vite. Vite." Then, when I caught up with him, he turned to me, and said quite deliberately in French: "Come with me, do what I say, and I will get you away to England." I felt that my prayer had been speedily answered.

TWELVE

Miracles Do Happen

Mangepin said that gendarmes were combing the district for me following a complaint from the owner of one of the barns into which I had broken: all the houses in Port Racine were being searched and everyone questioned. He thought that for the present I should stay hidden in the bracken on the hillside overlooking the harbour, an idea to which I agreed without demur. So we took a hillside track, he was leading the way, and soon arrived at the place he had in mind. There he pointed to a spot where the bracken was particularly thick and said I was to hide myself in it and remain out of sight and not move until evening when he would return: he would identify himself with a cry which he demonstrated. "Epp. Epp.—Kepp. Kepp.—Epp. Epp," he called and made me repeat it. When

135

I heard him in the evening I should make the same call in recognition.

It was not uncomfortable on the cliff top, lying on a scented mattress of bracken, shaded from the midday sun, and hidden by the bracken screen all round me which I had made thicker in parts. But in the afternoon time began to drag, and I had a struggle to restrain myself from getting up and having a look round; I did in fact once crawl a little way through the bracken, but I dare not go too far for fear of losing my way back to the hiding place. But I saw nothing of interest. After what seemed an eternity, darkness at last began to fall, but Mangepin did not return, and I began to have second thoughts about having trusted him. Perhaps he was, after all, in league with the gendarmes, I thought, and even at this moment leading them to my hiding place, though why he should make it all so complicated I was not calm enough to think out.

At last, however, I heard his strange recognition cry, which sounded exactly like some bird that I had heard often on my walks but could not put a name to. I answered it with the same high-pitched note and full vigour, feeling glad at the idea of action of any sort, good or bad. Standing up, I saw Mangepin pass my hiding place, and without stopping, continue at a fast pace down the hillside. I followed him closely, and soon we were both safely out of sight in the shelter of his cottage by the harbour, not far from the jetty. There were only a few others nearby, most of whose occupiers I knew, and I felt reasonably secure once we were inside.

Mangepin prepared a meal for me, and as I ate, he outlined the plans he had made on my behalf. They gave me a shock straightaway, for he proposed that I should try to escape in one of the two tiny home-made-looking boats I had seen in the harbour previously—a gimcrack affair only about 6 or 7 feet long, and with little more than a square yard of sail. It was an ideal means, no doubt, for picking up crab pots and nets in the shelter of the bay; but the thought of facing the Channel waves in it filled me with horror. There was another thing against it as far as I was concerned. It belonged to the fisherman whose wife had given me the needle, and who I had come to know well. He was pathetically poor, the boat his only means of livelihood, used for fishing in the bay, but never beyond. I suspected that he and Mangepin were not on good terms, and fleetingly I wondered if this had anything to do with the idea, in which case I might be the unwitting instrument for harming someone for whom I had developed great affection. It could, of course, be argued that my presence in the village constituted a danger to everyone in it, and that one man's loss was well worth getting me out of it; but on second thoughts I did not believe that Mangepin would think like that. After all, he had come at great personal risk to warn me I was in danger; and it was true that no other boat was at present available with sails. I did not want him to think I was ungrateful for what he had done, nor uncooperative, and so after considerable discussion I agreed to go along with his plan. Then, before we went to bed, he produced a bottle of rum and with its aid I slept soundly.

Mangepin's cottage had two stories, the top floor being used as a store and clothes drying room, as was normal in the area. The bed in the fishermen's cottages, indeed with country folk generally, is usually downstairs in the living room and is the most important piece of furniture in the house: even in the smallest homes it was often of grandiose design and size. I slept upstairs however, and was quite comfortable on some straw and matting. Mangepin roused me early next morning, and told me to stay out of sight during the day. Presently I heard footsteps and voices in the street below, and looking through the window could just see gendarmes standing at his front door. They did not stay, however, or enter the house; but soon after their departure, Mangepin crept silently up to me and whispered that they had been enquiring after me. He had told them he could not help: he had not seen me for some time.

During the rest of the day we discussed his plan in detail, working out the times of the tide, and the hour at which I should depart. In order to avoid the dreaded Blanchart Race, it was necessary to sail either at high or low tide, and to be well away from land before it changed. Mangepin recommended starting a little before low tide, which would give me the maximum possible time to get clear of the danger area; further, when the tide changed, it would be running in the right direction for me, eastwards up the Channel.

We finally decided that I should set out at 12 o'clock that night. During the evening we both slept for a while, and when roused by an alarm clock. I felt more than a little reluctant to get up; the enterprise I was about to embark on, as seen from the viewpoint of a warm bed, promised only great discomfort and a very dubious outcome. I did not think of calling it off, but I decided that if the boat proved as unseaworthy as I anticipated, I would find an excuse to return to Port Racine without delaying too long.

Mangepin insisted on coming to the beach to see me off; as we made our way slowly along the path to the jetty I could see about 50 yards away the glowing ends of the cigarettes of the German soldiers manning the gun detachment deployed at the cliff edge above the harbour. We reached the beach safely, then with my heart in my mouth, crossed the shingle to the water's edge, and soon located the cluster of boats tied up near the harbour entrance. It then took only a few minutes to untie the boat Mangepin had chosen for me, the smallest in the harbour, and to put aboard my food and water. Finally, in silence, we embraced, and I pushed off, using the oar over the stern like a gondolier (the French call it 'en godillant') so as to make as little noise as possible.

The wind was light, variable from the west. But the sail of

the miserable little craft proved almost useless, and I was taken on a trip round the bay before I could head towards the open sea; and as soon as I managed to get clear of the bay, the choppy waves broached and pooped the tiny boat. It was clear almost at once that I would never reach England in her. So without further delay I turned about and, the sail proving even more useless than it had at first, rowed most of the way back, all the time conscious of the sentries on the cliff whose lighted cigarettes were never out of sight. Finally I was back at the mooring from where I had started, and I tied up, thankful I had managed to return before dawn, and to tell the truth immensely relieved at not having to face the English Channel in such an unlikely craft.

Not too downcast, therefore, I stole back to Mangepin's house, and tapped lightly on the window. He let me in, at first seeming pleased to see me; but after a while his manner became cooler. To justify my return, I told him the wind had dropped completely; probably he did not believe me, but be that as it may, my earlier doubts about him returned with redoubled force as I observed his annoyance. Could I trust someone who expected me to take such fearful risks, I thought, courting almost certain death? If I could not, then the only alternative remained as before; give up the attempt to sail the Channel, and make tracks for the south and Spain.

Sleep was out of the question, although it was still night, and Mangepin and I sat arguing till dawn about what to do next. Surely, I said, there must be a bigger boat somewhere I could get hold of. Then almost as an afterthought, as if making conversation, I added that what I would most prefer would be to take M. Manime's motor launch—if only there were some petrol! In fact I did not really intend this to be taken seriously, but after I had spoken, Mangepin stared at me silently for a long time without saying anything, and I assumed he was treating my remark with justified contempt and ignoring it. Then out of the blue he said: ''But there is some petrol," and went on to explain that petrol at a special price was supplied by the gendarmes to the fishermen. On our way to the boat earlier in the evening we had passed only a few yards from a crate of petrol cans hidden in the bushes.

I began to wonder if I were losing my grip on reality. First Mangepin had proposed that I attempt to sail to England in a cockleshell boat which was barely fit to take round the bay, now he was telling me there was a motor boat with petrol available, and that he'd known about it for days. It just did not add up. Then some further questions began to trouble me. How was it that the petrol had not been already used by someone else? And how could we be sure it would remain untouched until I could collect it that evening? I pressed Mangepin for some explanations and found his replies so confident, and yet so vague, that I wondered if he really was alone in helping me. Were others, perhaps even M. Manime himself, in the business too, working with him to aid my escape? He gave no hint as to that then, or later, and I never found out. There was, of course, no good reason why he or anyone else should engage in such compromising activities on behalf of a lone survivor of an apparently defeated army. But a great deal that happened to me defied rational explanation.

Meanwhile, however, I was so uplifted with joy at this wonderful news that I soon ceased to worry myself with these doubts and quibbles. I told Mangepin that I would definitely leave in M. Manime's motor boat that night. My first concern was to ascertain that the petrol was still there and I asked Mangepin to check and he presently returned to say that it was still intact; then he described to me its exact location, so that in due course that night I should be able to find it without difficulty in the dark. The cans each held two litres, and were packed, he said, in a wooden crate which had been partly opened, so that they could be easily extracted. I asked how many he thought I should need to cross to England, and he replied that two should do; but I made a mental note to take three to be on the safe side.

I remained in the loft, and during the afternoon had a bad fright. While resting, I chanced to look out of the window and saw Manime's launch leaving the harbour with two German soldiers on board. I wondered anxiously if the enemy had got wind of my plans and if this was their way of check-mating me, by taking the launch away! But to my unbounded relief the launch returned about two hours later, and the Germans tied it up at its usual place at the jetty, the mooring allowing it to remain afloat even at low tide. I was greatly elated, for now I knew that the engine was in good working order. I only hoped that it had not been immobilised in a similar way to that used on motor cars, by removing the rotor arm from the distributor, but as I did not know whether a marine engine had a rotor arm, and even less where to look for it, it was a profitless speculation. Apart from that slight anxiety, my spirits now were soaring. After all the disappointments and false starts of the last five weeks, I felt sure that the big chance of which I had almost despaired had now finally come.

I realised of course that there were many difficulties still to be overcome before I was safely out of France, not least the danger of being heard as I carried provisions and petrol to the boat and stowed them aboard. They would have to be taken down an almost vertical iron ladder from the top of the jetty to the launch which, I was glad to confirm, was directly at the bottom of the ladder. I calculated that I should have to make two journeys at least, the first with provisions, the second with petrol, one can in each hand and a third tucked under an arm; which seemed to leave only my teeth with which to grasp that ladder!

In one important respect I was much better equipped than on my previous trip, for now I had a liquid compass, which Mangepin had given me. It was one of his most precious possessions, and after this generous gesture I again began to revise my opinion of him. Once I had explained exactly what I wanted he nearly always managed to find the right answer, producing each item with the merest glimmer of a smile.

Nevertheless he grew steadily more nervous as the day went by, and presently told me that in the evening I must move out of his house to the home of a relative, closer, he explained, to the footpath I should have to use when it was time to go, and easier to negotiate in the dark. It would be madness, he added in further explanation, to set out from the same house twice on successive nights, especially as I might have been seen returning in the early hours of the previous one.

At night-fall he took me to the house and introduced me to the owner, a pleasant old lady, who gave me a smile of welcome, although I thought she too looked rather strained. Then he said that he had done all he could for me and that now I must look after myself. Don't forget to set the alarm clock he added, handing it to me. Then he wished me good luck and for the second time we bid each other an emotional farewell, shaking hands warmly and embracing.

After he had gone, the old lady of the house told me that she also was leaving; but before doing so she gave me a thermos flask of hot coffee for the voyage, and pointed to some cold food on the table, which she said was for me. A bed was also made up for me to use while I waited for the time I was to go. She gave me a new word in the French language to puzzle over and try to interpret: she hoped I would soon 'désembrouillez'[1] myself; I translated this as disembroil myself, and I imagined, perhaps unfairly, that she hoped I would soon 'get out of their hair'. On further reflection I found a deeper meaning to the expression as it applied to my situation. It seemed to sum up all I had been

[1] I have never discovered an accepted English translation of the word. It is not given in any dictionary I have seen, even though it would seem to be used in ordinary speech.

trying to do for the last two months, just to disengage! In any case I bore no resentment at the expression being applied to me, since it was perfectly understandable in the light of the danger the whole community would have been exposed to if the Germans had discovered that even one or two people had actively helped me.

I had a good meal, then settled down and slept well until Mangepin's alarm clock woke me at 2.30 in the morning. I woke with a start, its clangour sounding ominous in my ears, like a knell calling me from a snug bed to a watery grave; but I soon forgot the cheerlessness of my solitary rising in the excitement of action.

Fortunately it was a dark, cloudy night, ideal for my purpose. Taking my bag, now heavier with the compass (it was in a wooden box about 9 inches square) and the thermos, I crept along to the end of the jetty and down the iron ladder to the boat which, as I had fervently hoped, was afloat some twelve feet or so below the top of the jetty, and lying quite close to the bottom of the ladder. It was a simple job to get hold of the mooring line and draw the boat gently up to the ladder and secure it. All the way, as before, I could see the glowing tips of cigarettes being smoked by the German sentries on the cliffs above; they were directly opposite and seemed very close, but how providential that they had not chosen to control the harbour at close quarters! Any slight noise, a scraping on the jetty wall, or something dropped into the water, would still alert them on the cliff, since it would have been magnified by reflection off the stone wall. For this reason I decided to make three separate trips up and down the ladder, carrying only one petrol can each time, after I had safely stowed the tarpaulin bag in the boat. Because the boat was afloat I did not this time have to walk across the shingle to reach it, and I managed to get the petrol aboard without being heard and without dropping any on the way down. At this stage I was still half bemused by my good fortune in finding the crate of petrol cans exactly as had been described to me, concealed in the long grass. Now I had managed three cans successfully, I was sorely tempted to go back for a few more to make doubly sure there was enough and to have a reserve. But I thought better of it. I might endanger everything by running any further risks and it was better to get away at once while the going was so unbelievably good.

Climbing aboard as silently as I could, I released the mooring line and cast off, then unshipped the oar and started sculling gently from the stern as I had the previous night, moving the oar sideways left and right, and at the same time swivelling it, to propel the boat forward. In this way I eased my way through the harbour entrance and out into clear water, not making any sound but leaving that tell-tale line of phosphorescent bubbles astern as before. In the darkness I was pretty confident I was not likely to be seen, although the lighted cigarettes of the German gun-site sentries were still clearly visible. Just what I would do if challenged I had not worked out, and I refused now to consider it. The very tranquillity of the scene was reassuring, and my confidence grew as the outline of the harbour wall slid past. Soon I was in the open sea, but I knew I must resist the temptation to have a go at starting the motor for at least half an hour. Meanwhile I continued to ease the boat forward with the oar, and tried not to think what might happen if I could not start the motor at all. To take my mind off this unpleasant possibility, I concentrated on thinking of the good Mangepin standing at his cottage window, straining to hear the sounds that would assure him of the success of what in truth was a joint venture, his and mine. He had intended to set his alarm clock at 2.30, the same time as mine; now the hands would be pointing roughly to 3.15. I imagined him wondering if the Englishman was going to disappoint him yet again, and return with his tail between his legs, the problem of what to do with him still unsolved. And then I imagined, in fancy, his ears would catch the faint note of a distant motor whispering across the water, and he would know I was on my way.

After half an hour's paddling I reached the far side of a rock which projected from the headland where the Napoleonic fort was in which I had sheltered; this, I thought would act as a sound barrier between the boat and the harbour, making it safe to try the motor. The moment of truth had come. I switched on and swung the handle, and the engine started at the first attempt.

I had not really expected such good fortune immediately and was overjoyed, as I thought again of Mangepin. Now I imagined him catching the sound, relaxing with a wide smile, and creeping back to his bed. Tomorrow, I thought, he would be able to tell the gendarmes that he had done what they wanted. For now that I was on my way, I felt sure that it was they who had made my escape possible, although it may well have been at Mangepin's suggestion. In any case, but for him, the attempt could not have been carried through; and I shall always be tremendously in his debt.

The ease with which the engine had started seemed to me a sign that fortune was on my side at last. Very excited I opened up the motor, and at full speed set a course due north, using the really efficient compass Mangepin had given me, which could be read in a second. When dawn broke I was well out into the Channel, the only indication of land being a distant barrage balloon behind me. It looked familiar, and was almost certainly one of ours that the Germans had taken over. The boat began to seem precariously small, and soon was tossing violently as we met the heavy seas of the open Channel; to make matters worse, a gale-force wind presently developed. And then the engine began to splutter and before long sounded as if it was going to peter out. I assumed it was running short of fuel, so I opened one of the petrol cans and tried to empty it into the fuel tank. This, however, proved extremely difficult: the wind blew much of the precious spirit overboard in a fine spray as I poured, resulting in the loss of a good third of the can. But the engine revived and we continued again to make good progress.

Then two Henschel reconnaissance planes appeared flying low and soon, the pilots spotting me, flew straight at me, dived across my bows several times and turned back towards the coast at full speed. The boat carried a small white pennant on the bowsprit, an identification mark indicating surrender which the Germans had ordered to be shown on all craft, and this I hoped had satisfied them that all was in order, although I was far outside the permitted fishing limits. At any rate, they did not shoot me up; but I wondered what would happen when they reported their sighting to base. I knew that some squadrons of Messerschmitts were stationed at Cherbourg and other places along the coast, and I feared the idea of a flight of them being despatched to deal with me.

As time went on and no Messerschmitts appeared, this fear receded and was replaced by a more pressing one, that of my petrol running out. I had to use the last of my three cans when, according to my reckoning, I was only about half way across the Channel, and it was by then clear that I could not hope to complete my journey under power. The wind meanwhile had strengthened from the northeast, and increasingly I could see a danger of being blown southwest which would take me right out into the Atlantic. The more I considered it, the more probable it seemed. I had no mast and no sail, and without power would be entirely at the mercy of the elements. My only chance of making a landfall would be a change in the wind; but even if it changed, I might continue to drift back and forth in the open sea for days . . . It was not a pleasant prospect.

How long I sat pondering an answer to this sombre problem I do not know. Occasionally the engine would splutter briefly; and then it stopped. I soon discovered the cause: the air filter connection had come adrift, as a result of which water was entering the air inlet. I managed to effect a repair by jamming the loose connections together with a piece of rag, and then succeeded in restarting the engine. But after a little while, it began to slow down again for a different reason: the fuel tank was nearly empty, and I had no reserve petrol left. As the afternoon wore on, and with the engine only just turning, I began seriously to think there was no alternative other than accepting defeat. It was a bitter pill, to fail so near home after struggling for so long and overcoming so many daunting obstacles. But as the last of my petrol was consumed and the engine almost at its last gasp, I was forced to accept that I had no hope of reaching England, or even of staying alive. I committed my soul to God, and considered ways of securing a quick deliverance from the horror of a long drawn out death in the wastes of the Atlantic.

It was then that I thought once more of the medallion which Mme Gemmetel had pinned on my shirt; I took it out of my pocket, and holding it in my hand, prayed for aid to our Lady of Lourdes, gazing the while at her image on the medallion. And a few minutes later, a seagull alighted on the boat's foredeck.

Because of its pitching and rolling, the bird had great difficulty in maintaining a footing, but balancing itself with the aid of its wings it succeeded in remaining with me for a few moments. Then it flew off, and alighted on the water a short distance ahead. Was it, I wondered, a sign to me not to give way to despair and to keep trying? The seagull flew up each time I reached it and flew on a short distance ahead and came down again as before on the surface; a process it repeated several times. It was trying to tell me something I felt sure and it could only be a message of encouragement. Whether or not seagulls have a special meaning for sailors I do not know, but it undoubtedly did restore my spirits and, more important, left me once more with the determination to apply rational thought to the situation, and to get out of the stupor into which I had sunk.

The engine, however, was by now labouring badly, and the boat making practically no way through the water; until finally it stopped altogether. But with my new determination I decided there were still things I could do, and seizing the oar I jammed it into the tube shaft of the boat's pump into which by good fortune it fitted, and then emptied my tarpaulin sack, opened it out flat, and succeeded in making a square sail of it by lashing sticks along the top and bottom edges. That done, I managed to fix it on the top end of the upright oar, and set it to catch the wind. My canvas sheet looked more like a distress signal than a sail—as indeed it was—but it worked, and by tacking, I succeeded after a while to get on to a northwest course. Once under way I found I was able to restart the engine which seemingly had enough fuel left to operate with the aid of the impulsion from the sail, and which then continued to run quite smoothly although very slowly. In this manner I carried on for quite a while, my seagull still keeping me company, moving in short flights, and continuing to come down frequently on the water ahead of me, and taking off again as soon as I caught up with it.

I was still making steady progress in the afternoon, when two Bristol Blenheims of the RAF flew past, travelling fast due north, and seemingly only just above the waves. This was the first sign that I might at last be entering friendly territory. And then some time later, I saw a white speck on the horizon to the north, and my heart gave a leap. Could it possibly be St Catherine's Point on the Isle of Wight, I wondered.

Slowly the speck became more distinct, and as the sun began to set I could see quite clearly that it was indeed the cliffs of the Isle of Wight that I was approaching. My journey was nearly over: I had escaped from German-occupied Europe.

The boat's engine continued to run slowly until, in the half light of dusk, I could clearly distinguish the cliff face ahead of me. When finally it stopped, I took down my sail and started to row, spurred by visions of the comfortable hotel at Freshwater Bay which I had visited in peace-time and which I knew must now be close. But then the tide turned, and soon the cliff face was slipping rapidly away eastwards as I was carried helplessly by the current, which was too strong to row against. Though I did not know it at the time, this proved a blessing in disguise for in the area where I had expected to land the beaches were all mined: something I should have thought of but hadn't.

Alum Bay slipped past, followed quickly by the Needles; and then again I was out of sight of land. As it grew dark, the wind dropped but backed to the southeast, so I put up my makeshift sail once more and during the night coaxed the boat as best I could on a northerly course, although I seemed to achieve little if any movement through the water.

When dawn broke I found that I was somewhere between Poole and Christchurch, and about midway between the mainland and the Isle of Wight. The sun was already up when a coasting vessel, the first I had seen during the whole of my trip, passed some distance away. I took down my sail and using it as a signal flag, waved frantically to attract attention but without result. No one aboard saw me, or if they did, just ignored me. Deeply disappointed, I went back to the job of trying to steer north.

And then I saw in the distance a Royal Navy patrol boat coming in my direction, and this time I got both the oar and canvas out to wave rather turgidly as a signal flag, spelling out SOS in morse. The signal seemed to have registered, and after what seemed an eternity, MV *Aquamarine* approached and then spent some time manoeuvring near enough to throw me a line. Finally contact was made, and grasping the line I managed to pull myself alongside.

I was helped up on deck where the captain was waiting to find out what he had picked up. He began by asking what nationality I was, and was clearly amazed when I told him I was a British Army officer who had been taken prisoner in France and had escaped and was returning home. I went on at once to express my warm thanks to him for taking notice of my SOS and for coming to pick me up. I felt a little deflated, however, when he replied that he was on his way to investigate me in any case. The unusual clinker-built style of the hull of the boat, apparently typical of French craft, had caught his eye and made him decide to find out more.

A few more enquiries, and then came a wonderful question: Would I like a bath and some breakfast? Please, I said with a broad smile. With the solid feel of the deck under my feet, and the early prospect of bacon and eggs and hot tea, I felt that I was really home at last. Before I went below I asked that my boat be taken in tow back to their Isle of Wight base at Yarmouth; this I was told had already been taken care of.

Shortly after I was picked up, an enemy aircraft dropped a stick of bombs between us and the western tip of the Isle of Wight. This was the only reception honour I was accorded on my arrival; if I could have been sure that it was the result of the report made by the Henschel pilots who had buzzed me the previous morning, my day would have been complete. It was Thursday, 1st August 1940, a date forever in my calendar.

Later in the morning I was landed at the Naval Base at Yarmouth and then taken to the HQ of the local Army defence force. Telephone wires had been humming meanwhile; news of my arrival had been sent first to Area HQ at Portsmouth, thence to a Southern Command, and finally on to the War Office, who replied that an officer would be detailed to escort me to London.

On arrival at the Army HQ on the Isle of Wight I was

shown to the officers' mess, where, understandably, I caused quite a sensation. I was welcomed very hospitably by the CO and his officers and several of them started to ask me questions about my experiences. I did my best to answer, occasionally finding that I was talking in French, but the CO quickly intervened, and said I should say nothing until the man from the War Office arrived.

I could not even be allowed to go out to do some shopping, until he turned up. When he did, about an hour later, however, he agreed to accompany me to the Post Office, where he allowed me to send a telegram to my wife, who, in early June had been informed that I was reported missing, presumed killed, and was already in receipt of her army widow's pension. Then I did a little shopping, my purchases including for some peculiar reason a cloth cap. Perhaps I wanted to conceal my uncombed, unkempt hair. Then my escort, a major, took me by ferry to Portsmouth, thence in a car to Southern Command at Wilton near Salisbury, and finally on to the War Office in London.

I arrived there still wearing my French farmer's blue jersey and tatty old trousers, and continued to wear them for several days before I was finally kitted out with a new uniform. On the first day I was not allowed out of the War Office, nor was I left alone at all, and I had a feeling that I was suspected of not being what I said I was. My standing was probably not improved when I asked permission to telephone my home and then could not remember the number. Continuing doubts about my *bona fides* were probably the cause of the consternation a day or two later, when I was allowed to go to a Regent Street tailor to be measured for a new uniform, and was away half an hour or so longer than expected. When I returned I was required to give chapter and verse about all my movements. It was possibly for the same reason that I was not allowed to go to my home in Surrey, some 23 miles from London for a week, during which I was questioned every day by officers from various Military and Naval Intelligence departments, and in between dictated my story to an Army shorthand writer. I had to stay at a hotel in London the while, though my wife, who was pregnant (she gave birth to twins three and a half weeks later) was allowed to visit me there.

At last, however, the War Office told me I was free to go home for a short leave, to join my wife and family, and to meet my neighbours. I was greeted as a man back from the dead—and for some while I felt like one.

THIRTEEN

Second Thoughts with Hindsight

Anyone who, under whatever pressures, has put at risk the lives of others, particularly strangers, must live with an unresolved question of guilt. Certainly in war-time, circumstances can conspire to render such risks virtually unavoidable, when, as in my case, one's presence as an escaper prompted so many ordinary people voluntarily to risk incurring the severest penalties for helping me.

When, in 1946, I returned with my wife to Normandy, and met again those good people, the Gemmetels and Beauchaux, I found myself deeply intrigued by their simple and straightforward attitude as they recalled, very vividly, what they had lived through at the hands of the gendarmes and Gestapo in their efforts to implicate them in my escape. They had stoutly denied any knowledge of my true identity

153

or intentions, choosing to remember me as the refugee from the North, with a Flemish mother and a consequent vile accent.

In the case of M. Manime the Cherbourg dentist, in whose boat I had escaped, I was distressed to hear that he had died in 1945 after being imprisoned and terribly ill-treated by the Gestapo—perhaps on suspicion of being an accessory in allowing his craft to be taken, but more probably, it appeared, for regularly listening to the banned BBC broadcasts.

Strange as I had found his ambivalent attitude I was never really satisfied about a link between him, as owner of the boat and the so-handy petrol, and the well-informed fisherman Mangepin, who had no reason at all to be so staunch in the assistance and encouragement he gave me.

Mere words of thanks in such cases are feeble but have to be expressed, as indeed does my gratitude to the Royal Navy for so efficiently ensuring that M. Manime's boat was returned in good order to his family after the war.

I am not likely to forget my debt to the Captain and crew of MV *Aquamarine* who picked me up, to the other members of the Senior Service who helped me when I first landed, a veritable scruffy landlubber, and to the Army authorities on the Isle of Wight who looked after me so well in their Mess. And a special thank you to the officer who gave me his raincoat as I boarded the ferry to Portsmouth in the pouring rain.

On that visit to Port Racine with my wife in 1946, I took her to the Anse St Martin so that I could show her exactly where I had beached the sailing boat in which I made my first unsuccessful attempt to sail to England. To my amazement the hull planks of the craft were still visible there, buried in the shingle exactly where, "comme une vache", I had beached it, six years and a world war before.

FOURTEEN

Aftermath

After my return I received a flood of letters which continued for several months, mostly congratulatory, some making enquiries about relations or friends who had been taken prisoner at the same time as I was, and making comments on one aspect or another of my experiences. In a few cases I was able to give the writers good news, and I arranged to meet a few others so that I could tell them at first hand what I knew. But there were so many letters that I was unable to answer them all, and to this day I feel a sense of guilt about those to which I did not reply.

Some of my correspondents asked questions about the men who joined my mixed body of troops and stragglers at the farm in the early days of the German attack. Several of them were from the Rifle Brigade and the Queen Victoria

Rifles, who were rushed from England to Calais at the last minute to try to save the port from capture; all without their motor transport and in particular the motorcycle and sidecar combinations which were their distinctive standard issue. It was thought at the time that this was the result of the equipment having been sent over in a different ship and separated from the men in the general confusion at Calais, where some units were being evacuated while others were simultaneously arriving. Subsequent reports by Rifle Brigade and QVR personnel who managed to get back to England suggest however that an alternative reason for the missing transport equipment may have been the refusal of the dockers on the quayside to off-load the supply ship.

One of the major factors contributing to the collapse of France in 1940 was Germany's treaty of friendship with the Soviet Union which served to neutralise much of the anti-German feeling of the French working class. The effects of this were far reaching, extending into the civil service as well as the fighting forces, and giving the German's fifth column wide-ranging opportunities to manipulate officials, organise confusion and spread false information.

The complete breakdown of communications which occurred can also be attributed in large part to this cause. The lack of reliable information about the movements of the BEF in the course of their retreat northwards, and the contradictory reports received by the Commander in Chief, Lord Gort, and by the Cabinet in London, because of the breakdown, all contributed to the débâcle. In my opinion, the Soviet Friendship Treaty was one of the most important successes of German strategy in the early days of the war. It was of course discarded as soon as it had served its purpose.

One letter of particular interest came nearly a year after my return to England. It was from the secretary of the Jersey Society in London, who wrote that he had heard about my escape from a mutual friend and was extremely interested in the references to Jersey in my story, especially the account of my arrival off St Helier and discovering that the island was under German occupation. He went on to say that the committee of the Society would very much like me to give a talk about my experiences at one of their forthcoming meetings.

I wrote back saying that I should be happy to oblige, providing I got clearance from the War Office, and I had several letters from the Secretary subsequently—I have them still—written over a period of a year or more. But sadly arrangements could never be finalised, partly because I was posted to the Middle East in 1942. In his last letter, dated June of that year and sent after I had already left Britain, the Secretary asked if the lecture was ready and enquired, if I was abroad, whether it could be read for me by someone else. He went on: "there was a persistent rumour going round Jersey for some time after the German occupation started that some fishermen employed by the Germans had seen an Englishman in a boat in which he had escaped from France off the Corbieres; that he was about to land in Jersey, but that they warned him that the Germans were there, and he then went away. There can be little doubt that this story refers to you."

In the same letter the Secretary referred to the escape of a man from Jersey which had taken place the previous autumn, that is in 1941. His story, he went on, "is not unlike yours, for he made one attempt and spent four days on an isolated reef before being compelled by storms and an attack of influenza to return home. Many months later he made a second and successful attempt, and being deprived of food, water and the use of his engine through accidents, finally in the course of three days rowed practically the whole distance and suffered, as I understand you did, extreme privations and vivid hallucinations."

I should dearly have liked to compare notes about the hallucinations with this other escaper, and to find out whether he thought they really were hallucinations or, as I thought, actual objects seen bathed in the wonderful golden red glow of sunrise, when seen off St Helier. Perhaps he saw such things and believed them to be figments of his imagination, or perhaps he had quite different experiences. It would have been interesting to know.

One picture stays obstinately in my mind even to this day from among all the events of this story. That is the look on the face of the French Naval officer when last seen making his escape from the farm at Marcq where we had arrested him on suspicion of being not only a fifth columnist but a potential saboteur on his way to the UK via Dunkirk. He and a fellow French officer had turned up at our reserve HQ in the woods in a small unmarked van. Like all who came into our camp out of the blue, they were questioned. Our suspicions strongly aroused we asked them to unlock their suitcases, even though they both assured us they had nothing to cause suspicion. They refused to comply on the excuse that they had lost the keys. We shot the locks off and on lifting the lid found, right at the top, a number of large-scale British army ordnance maps of the Aldershot district and a quantity of English money. The maps had various cryptic markings at several points. They had previously told us they had got away from one of the forts in the Calais port citadel but how they had managed to load all their luggage was far from clear since it included bulky items such as a sextant, liquid compass and so on. They were at once told that they were under strict arrest and liable to be shot if they attempted to escape. In spite of this after a short while they both made a bolt for it and one was shot. The other, however, contrived to sidle off into some bushes, giving me a curiously intent look as he went. He disappeared into the dusk and eluded our search parties. This was about the 24th May which was just a day or two before Hitler's famous order to halt the Panzer attack on Dunkirk. Military historians generally agree that this order saved over 300,000

British troops which would otherwise had been trapped, and gave Britain a chance to reorganise and continue the fight. Why he gave this order has never been satisfactorily explained even by German generals in their memoirs. But it was in the ultimate analysis the basic reason why Hitler lost the war. It is too fanciful to think that the treatment of the two disguised agents at our hands at Marcq could have been reported to German HQ, but it must be remembered that there was an active fifth column cell at the village as I discovered later. However, it could also add a new dimension to the meaning of 'Disembroil' in the sense of opposing fifth column infiltration and sabotage embroilment. Instead of the buck stops here, why not 'The Disembroill starts here' as the motto on the wall?